ISBN 978-1-330-29433-8
PIBN 10016720




FB &c Ltd, Dalton House, 60 Windsor Avenue, London, SW19 2RR.
Company number 08720141. Registered in England and Wales.

For support please visit www.forgottenbooks.com

# URAL HARMONY

BY

FRANKLIN W. ROBINSON
*Head of the Department of Ear-Training and Dictation in the Institute of Musical Art, New York City*

PART I

G. SCHIRMER
NEW YORK · BOSTON

27815

RESPECTFULLY INSCRIBED AND DEDICATED TO

"L. G."

WHO HAS BEEN A CONSTANT SOURCE
OF INSPIRATION WHILE WRITING
THIS TREATISE ON AURAL
HARMONY.

# AUTHOR'S NOTE

After many years of experience in the teaching of harmony along the lines usually followed in presenting the subject, the author has come to feel an intense need for a presentation that would meet the demands of the lesser talent as well as the great talent — a presentation which would seek to edify the student by appealing to his musical consciousness through the ear, and by means of that experience to equip him with the power to hear what he writes.

The opportunity presented itself when the Institute of Musical Art, in New York City, came into existence; it is, therefore, with warmest gratitude that the author acknowledges, not only the kindness, but the unqualified trust which the director of the Institute, Dr. Frank Damrosch, has shown in permitting the initial presentation of aural harmony. The high standard of musical study, as carried on at the Institute of Musical Art, has been a great stimulus in working out and in bringing to fruition this new subject.

The author also wishes to extend his thanks to Mr. Thomas Tapper for his kindness in reviewing and criticising the subject-matter and the form of presentation of this book.

It is hoped that the treatise will be accepted in the spirit in which it has been written, namely, a sincere effort to present the subject of harmony in a more useful and tangible form and, thereby, to make it more applicable and adaptable to all the fields of musical experience.

FRANKLIN W. ROBINSON.

*New York, June, 1917.*

# PREFACE

A treatise on "harmony" should include three large divisions or "aspects":

(1) PHYSICS — laws governing the vibration of any sounding bodies, i.e., the science of acoustics.

(2) PHYSIOLOGY — an inquiry into the action of the ear in discerning sounds — the use of the ear in music.

(3) PSYCHOLOGY — the mental effects that resounding bodies have upon the mind — to impress the mind with the emotional qualities which chords and keys possess.

## 1. Physics

Concerning the first of these divisions, *viz.*, physics; much has been done in this field of tonal relationships. To this source the theorist of music should revert in order not to resort to arbitrary and didactic statements with regard to the relationship of chords or the formation of scales. There is much in the science of acoustics which is irrelevant to the task of writing a treatise on harmony. Discussions have arisen with regard to the tempered scale versus the natural scale, — with regard to the size of intervals as constant or varying, etc. Such discussions are irrelevant to the subject of harmony. The wisest course to pursue is to take that which is useful, and discard that which does not apply. Acoustical law should be utilized to prove the formation of the scale and to establish certain basic laws and principles of tonal relationship, thereby avoiding arbitrary rules and laws.

Music, as an art-form, is science idealized, not a tonal exposition of exact acoustical law. It is at this point that the ear, in its inconsistency in apprehending tonal relationship, determines that all intervals shall not necessarily be exactly (acoustically) perfect, and that the tempered fifth shall be the idealized interval which will make possible the interrelation of the fifteen different scales through the process of modulation.

All art takes into account the instability of the sense to which it appeals. If the art of music did not take into account the universal instability present in every human ear which hears all perfect fifth intervals as a little less than absolutely acoustically perfect fifths, then music would simply be the tonal exposition of a branch of physics called acoustics. The idealization of the perfect fifth does not affect the accuracy of the acoustical law in determining the relationship of tones or the construction of scales; no interval of a fifth is heard as *absolutely* perfect in music; if such a fifth in music were produced absolutely perfect, to satisfy the value of $x$ in the following equation

$$2 : 3 :: 256 : x$$

all normal musical ears would determine such an interval of a fifth as being out of tune, the upper tone of the perfect fifth becoming a little sharp in sound.

Therefore, the science of acoustics will be used to determine basic laws for all tonal relationships relating to scale-construction and chord-construction; beyond these limits it will not be employed.

## 2. Physiology

Concerning the second of the divisions, *viz.*, physiology as it relates to the action of the ear in discerning sounds. The human ear is so constituted as to take in many sounds at the same moment; it was meant to hear in the multiple, not singly, therefore in listening to music the ear should apprehend large masses of sound; the ear should act, in other words, in the ensemble. If a certain instrument is to be discerned by the ear when played in an orchestra, a definite mental state is necessary in order that the ear shall act to discern that particular instrument; allowed to follow its own normal trend, the ear will always act in the ensemble; it will act generically and not specifically. This fact makes for a basis of all method in presenting aural harmony.

Tones in music are never listened to as isolated tones (in

other words, as unrelated tones); they are always degrees of a scale, of a melody, or of a chord. A chord is not discerned by hearing all the single tones of which it is composed, but is heard in the ensemble as an entity built up upon a root-tone in a succession of thirds and related to the scale, of which it is a servant. The great fallacy in the use of the ear in music is the tendency to train it to hear isolated tones and isolated chords.

Music is tonal relationship built upon two laws:

(1) a basic law, namely, the *harmonic* law;

(2) a law derived from the harmonic law, namely, the *melodic* law.

Upon these two laws depend all the tonal relationships possible in music.

In the training of the ear in music, the tonal relationships determining the harmonic law, being basic, are discerned first; the tonal relationships determining the melodic law, being dependent upon the harmonic law, are discerned next.

All tones in music are related to each other through the medium of activity and rest. The degree of any scale is either a rest tone or an active tone; any chord of the scale is either a rest chord, or one of many active chords.

Play the scale of C and perceive the active quality of the tone B, the rest quality of the tone C or the tone G. The musical ear is quickly affected by these qualities; and, commensurable with the power of the ear to discern the active and rest qualities which tones possess, is a person considered musical. The ear is therefore trained (1) to listen to related tones and not to isolated tones; (2) to listen in the ensemble, and not to single tones; (3) to listen to tonal relationship through the medium of activity and rest as setting up two laws (harmonic and melodic) which make those tonal relationships purposeful and not merely pleasant sounding concords or melodies.

In formulating a method for the study of aural theory all of these points will be taken into consideration.

### 3. Psychology

Concerning the third division, psychology: Under this heading will be discussed the different emotional attributes of major and minor scales, perfect and imperfect intervals, consonant and dissonant intervals and chords, and diatonic and chromatic harmonies.

The psychological aspect of aural harmony is therefore the side that gathers all the subject-matter, acoustically built and physiologically discerned, and strives to make its use a purposeful use by reflecting upon the emotional aspects of musical phenomena and making thereby a language out of music; for example, a chromatic chord may be very beautiful and still be entirely inadequate to represent the subtle emotional meaning which is required of it.

It would therefore seem imperative that all scales, melodies, and chords (diatonic and chromatic), which, roughly speaking, is the subject-matter concerned in aural harmony, should be discussed with regard to their meaning in order that their use may become purposeful and filled with sense.

The psychological side of the study of aural harmony should be presented along with every phase of the subject as it is unfolded. It enters into the understanding of melody. Intervals must be aurally determined by the characteristic qualities which they possess; for example, the brightness of the major third versus the sombreness of the minor third; the static quality of a consonance versus the dynamic quality of a dissonance; the natural purity and strength of the diatonic chord versus the artificial emotional quality of the chromatic chord.

The psychological phase of the subject of harmony is therefore the natural resultant phase of the whole work; it develops the power of the mind to think *through* to a conclusion (therefore to a purposeful use) concerning all the phenomena of tonal relationships employed in music. Goethe once said, "We name everything under the sun, but know so little about anything." In order that the student of aural theory shall not at the end of his study become classified as one of those who can name all the scale-degrees, intervals and chords and still know nothing about them, it is sincerely hoped that this all-important phase of aural theory will be vigorously sought out and absorbed.

The power to concentrate through the use of the ear is another phase in the presentation of aural theory about which it is very necessary to be careful; the ear of the average musical person must be trained to listen according to law and therefore the ear must always be directed towards the discernment of tonal relationships, rather than towards the mere sound of tones which are in relationship; in other words, aural concentration consists in the power of the mind through the action of the ear to think the law which governs the tones which are heard. As a direct result of the *power to concentrate* through the ear and to *think through* a musical experience to make it purposeful, will come another, possibly the greatest, power of the musical mind, namely, to formulate a musical judgment. This would seem to be the aim and end of all musical study.

It is deemed advisable in closing to touch upon the subject of the method which will be employed in presenting aural harmony. There are two recognized methods of approaching any science or art:

(1) The Deductive Method.

(2) The Inductive Method.

The deductive method is the one employed by theorists in music, resulting in the statement of didactic laws and rules; and by the application of these laws and rules in the realm of tonal relations the phenomena of musical composition are derived and related.

The inductive method proceeds from another point of departure. It assumes the phenomena of tonal relationships as it finds them; then, by experience in using and relating them, it induces the laws which govern them. The musician starts with the belief that the laws underlying tonal relationships are ever present in nature as natural laws, and that in order to understand them he must seek them through experience.

The inductive method is believed to be the legitimate method of approach in writing a treatise on aural harmony; therefore, it is to be expected that all reasoning which ultimately results in the establishment of laws and rules, will spring from the experience of tonal phenomena, inducing from that experience the laws which govern those phenomena.

FRANKLIN W. ROBINSON.

*June 1, 1917*

# CONTENTS

Page

Preface . . . . . . . . . . . . . . . . . . . . . . . . . vi

PART I

Chapter

I. The Scale . . . . . . . . . . . . . . . . . . . . . 1

II. Intervals . . . . . . . . . . . . . . . . . . . . . 12

III. Chord-Construction, and the Triad . . . . 27

IV. The Use of the Primary Triads in Four-Part Writing 35

V. The Phrase as Determined by the Harmonic Relationship of the Primary Triads in Their Fundamental Positions . . . . . . . . . . . . . . . . . . 46

VI. Melody Harmonization of Melodies . . . . . . . 58

VII. The Secondary Triads in Major . . . . . . . . . . 66

VIII. The Period . . . . . . . . . . . . . . . . . . . 90

IX. Inversion of the Primary Triad . . . . . . . . . . 92

X. Inversions of the Secondary Triads . . . . . . . . 102

XI. Discords . . . . . . . . . . . . . . . . . . . . 112

XII. The Dominant Seventh-Chord . . . . . . . . . . . 117

XIII. Inversions of the Dominant Seventh-Chord 123

XIV. The Minor Mode . . . . . . . . . . . . . . . . . 137

XV. The Secondary Triads in Minor: Inversions of the Primary and Secondary Triads and the Dominant Chord . . . . . . . . . . . . . . . . . . . . . 147

XVI. Modulation: Modulation to the Nearest Keys . . . 157

XVII. Modulation to Remote (or Extraneous) Keys 177

XVIII. Further Development of Melody: The Accompaniment to Melody . . . . . . . . . . . . . . . . 191

XIX. Summary . . . . . . . . . . . . . . . . . . . . 196

# AURAL HARMONY

## PART I

## CHAPTER I

### THE SCALE

The simplest pitch-relationship known in music is the scale. A scale is the relationship in pitch of a succession of tones back to a *root*-tone, thereby involving a relationship of these tones to one another. The relationship of all of the tones of a scale to the root-tone is affirmed by determining the successive degrees of the scale by numeral names (1, 2, 3, 4, 5, 6 and 7). The relationship of the tones of a scale to one another is affirmed by the quality of rest or of activity which each tone possesses.

Let us assume the scale C as a typical scale. The root-tone C is the tone which names the scale; the tones C, D, E, F, G, A and B, being called also by their numerical names 1, 2, 3, 4, 5, 6 and 7, affirm the relationship of the several tones back to the tone C. The relationship of the adjacent tones of the scale of C to one another (*viz.*, F to E, A to G, B to C, D to E) is expressed through the medium of activity and rest. Play an octave of the scale of C and further establish the tonal feeling of the scale by playing in successsion its 1st, 3rd, 5th and 8th degrees. Sound the tone B, which is the 7th of the scale, and note its active tendency to proceed upward into the 8th degree of the scale; upon arriving at the 8th degree, note the rest quality of this tone. Do this likewise with the tone F (the 4th degree), and note its active tendency (though not so pronounced) to proceed downward into the tone E, which is the 3rd degree of the scale; note the rest quality of the 3rd degree. Do this likewise for the tone A (the 6th degree), and note its active tendency downward into the rest tone G, which is the 5th degree of the scale. Likewise the active tendency of the tone D in either direction (up or down) to the rest tones E (3rd degree), or the rest tone C (1st degree). This experiment establishes these facts:

(1) The adjacent tones of the scale are related to one another through the medium of activity and rest.

(2) The tonal feeling of the scale is set up by the active tones in seeking and proceeding to rest tones.

How does it come that the 1st, 3rd and 5th degrees of any scale are rest tones and that the 2nd, 4th, 6th and 7th degrees are active tones with a desire to resolve to the rest tones?

The answer to this question lies in the proof of the relationship of all of these six differing tones back to the root-tone. They all differ in pitch from the tone C, and still they are all related to C in pitch. Therefore what is sought, to prove their relationship to the tone C, is in reality a least common denominator in pitch, which, when applied out from the tone C, will derive the several tones (2nd, 3rd, 4th, 5th, 6th and 7th) of the scale. It is apparent that this least common denominator must be the product of a tone which is nearest related to the tone C and still differs in pitch from the tone C. A relationship in pitch between two tones is called an interval; therefore the least common denominator will be an interval, the upper tone of which is a tone in relation to C whose pitch is nearest related to the pitch of the tone C, and yet differs from it.

Let us now seek this least common denominator in pitch by assuming the tense medium of a stretched string so tuned as to resound the tone C. The least common denominator which is related to this tone (now represented by the tense string) will be the tone resulting from the simplest division of the stretched string which produces a tone differing from the tone C. The simplest division that the string can undergo is into halves. By such a division, a tone differing from tone C is not obtained, for it is found that both halves of the string sound a tone which has the same pitch as the tone resulting from the vibration of the whole string; the pitch resulting from the vibration of half of the string is, however, judged to be an octave higher; this tone resulting from the vibration of half of the string is therefore said to be the octave of the fundamental. Thus the octave of any tone is the same tone in a different place; in other words, changing the octave relationship of a tone does not change its pitch relationship. It merely changes its place relationship (called in music "register"). It is therefore apparent that the division of the string into halves does not serve to determine the least common denominator which is sought.

Ex. 1.

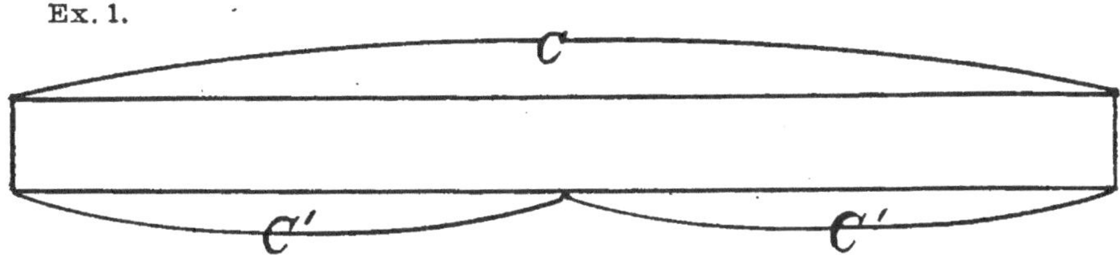


The next simplest division of the string is into thirds. It is easily discovered that the longer the vibrating medium the deeper is the tone resulting from the vibration. Therefore in dividing the string into thirds the vibration of the two-thirds length of the string would result in a tone more nearly approximating the tone resulting from the vibration of the full length of the string than if the one-third length were made to vibrate. The tone which results from vibrating the two-thirds length of the string is found to be G, which is the fifth of the scale of C and therefore forms with the tone C an interval called a fifth. (The name of an interval is determined along the scale of its lower tone, and its numerical name is always the degree-name of the upper tone along the scale of the lower tone.) Hence, the interval of a fifth is the least common denominator sought, inasmuch as the tone G, forming a fifth with the tone C, is a tone differing in pitch from C, and is, at the same time, the nearest related tone to C, resulting as it does from the simplest division of the string vibrating C.

Applying this least common denominator up and down from the tone C, we obtain (upward from C), first, the tone G; a fifth above G, the tone D; a fifth above D, the tone A; a fifth above A, the tone E; a fifth above E, the tone B; a fifth above B, the tone F#; a fifth above F#, the tone C#. This C# determines a limit to the application of the least common denominator in this direction, for the tone C♯, resulting a fifth above F♯, contradicts the key-tone C; and where there is contradiction there ceases to be relationship.

Applying the fifth downward from the key-tone C, the tone F results, which is seen to contradict the tone F♯, the last tone determined by applying the fifth above C. Which of these tones, F or F♯, shall be accepted as the legitimate fourth step of the scale of C? There seems to be no choice between the two tones judged merely from their derivation, and the selection would seem to rest upon the result of applying the least common denominator out from each of the tones, determining from the *resulting tones* which one contradicts the scale-tones already derived in the more forceful manner; for it would seem to be good reasoning that the tone from which the less contradicting tone is derived would by this fact affirm itself as being nearer related to the key-tone.

Ex. 2.

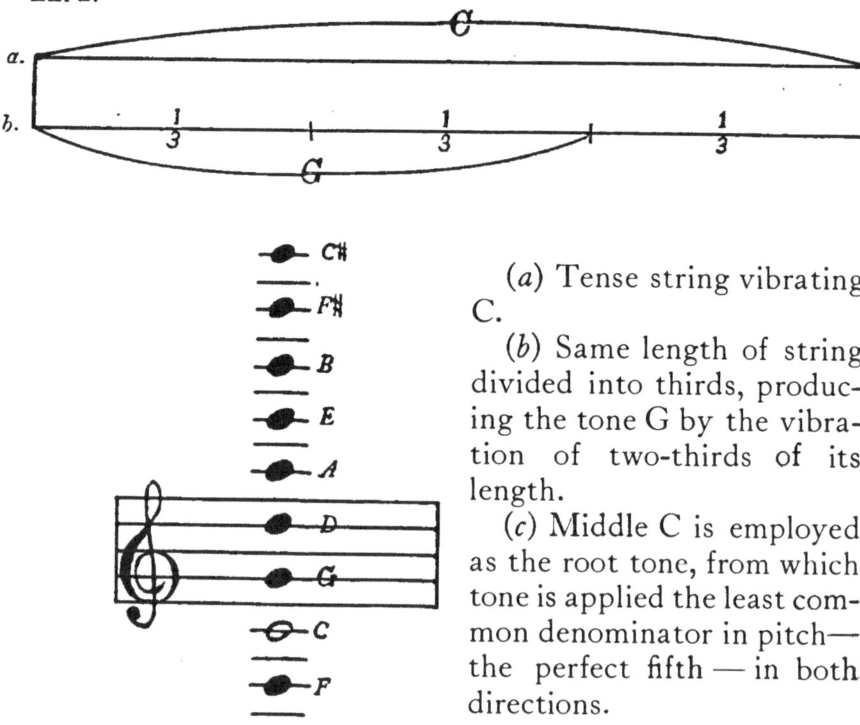


(*a*) Tense string vibrating C.

(*b*) Same length of string divided into thirds, producing the tone G by the vibration of two-thirds of its length.

(*c*) Middle C is employed as the root tone, from which tone is applied the least common denominator in pitch—the perfect fifth — in both directions.

From the tone F (proceeding downward in the application of the least common denominator) the tone B♭ is determined; this tone is a contradiction of the tone B already determined (which is the 7th degree or leading-tone, so called, of the scale), and although a contradiction of an important tone of the scale, it is by no means as keen a contradiction as the tone C♯ (which is a contradiction of the key-tone (C) is of the tone C. It follows, that the tone F takes precedence over the tone F♯ as a related tone to the key-tone C, and becomes the fourth degree of the scale of C.

In order to visualize the derivation of the several tones by the successive subdivisions of and additions to the string vibrating to produce the tone C, the following diagram is affixed.

Ex. 3.

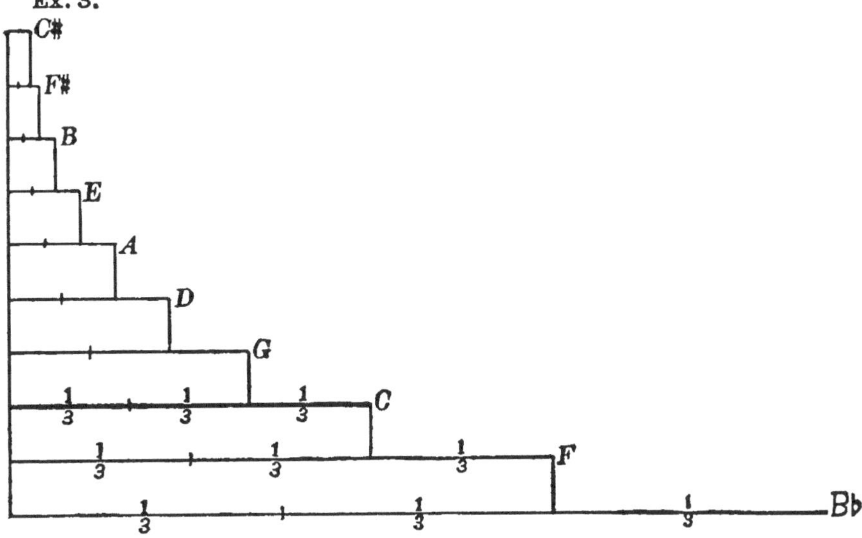


The original (heavy) line C is made the basis of the applica tion of the 2 : 3 relationship. By successively *dividing* the line-lengths into 3rds, starting with the line C, the tones G, D, A, E, B, F♯ and C♯ are obtained. By using the heavy line C as a two-thirds length and *adding* another third to it, the tone F results. Assuming this line F to be a two-thirds length, and adding another third, the tone B♭ results. It is thus seen that the heavy line C is in a relationship of 2: 3 with the line-lengths determining the tone F and the tone B♭ by the process of addition; whereas the heavy line C is in a relationship of 2 : 3 with the line-lengths determining the tones G, D, A, E, B, F♯ and C♯ by the process of division. In other words, the *relationship* 2 : 3 to obtain *all* of the tones, remains constant, but the *method* of application changes from one of *division* in obtaining G, D, A, E, B, F♯ and C♯, to one of *addition* in obtaining F and B♭.

This series of tones, springing initially from any key-tone, is called the *harmonic scale* of that key-tone. Therefore, the harmonic scale of C is C (key-tone), G, D, A, E, B, obtained by applying the perfect fifths *above* the key-tone; and the tone F by applying the perfect fifth below the key-tone.

Rearrange these tones so that they become adjacent to one another, by changing their octave positions (noting that the octave of a tone does not change its pitch relationship, but merely its place or register), the diatonic scale of C whose existence was sought is proved, and the manner in which these adjacent tones are related to the key-tone is established.

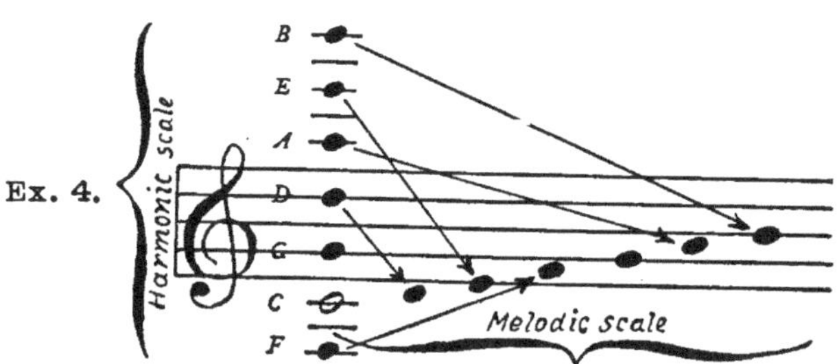


It follows, that the diatonic (or stepwise) scale of C is a rearranged relationship of the tones previously arranged in a perfect-fifth relationship. Such a diatonic scale of C is called the melodic scale of C.

In the harmonic scale of C all of the tones are derived out from the key-tone C, and because of this fact they are all disposed to resolve into the key-tone C. In other words, in the harmonic scale there is but one rest tone, namely the key-tone; all the other tones are active tones, their activity varying inversely as the square of their distance from the key-tone. The principle of activity here cited is most clearly discerned by imagining the key-tone to be a magnetic centre, and the other tones as being susceptible to the pulling power of this magnetic centre. In the harmonic scale of C the tone nearest the key-centre is the most active, namely the tone G. The next less active tone is the one a fifth above G, namely, D; the activity of the tone F, located below the tone C, is determined by placing it (where, experimentally, it will be found to be located) upon the 5th line of the staff between the tones D and A. This tone F is therefore the next less active tone after D; the tone A is the next less active tone; the tone E is the next less active tone; and the least active tone is B, being farthest away from the key-tone C.

*Therefore, the activity of every tone of the harmonic scale is inversely as the square of the distance of that tone from the key-tone: this statement is the scientific basis of the* **harmonic law** *of any scale.*

Turning from the contemplation of the activities of the tones of the harmonic scale to the activities of the melodic scale, it is seen at a glance that the activities of one scale do not determine the activities of the other scale; for the most active tone in the harmonic scale of C is the tone G, which tone in the melodic scale is a rest tone; the least active tone in the harmonic scale of C, namely, the tone B, is the most active tone in the melodic scale of C. It is also seen that the only rest tone in the harmonic scale is the key-tone. All the other tones are active tones, whereas in the melodic scale there are three rest tones, the key-tone, and the 3rd and 5th of the melodic scale. It has been stated above why the key-tone is the only rest tone of the harmonic scale; it is now fitting to inquire into the manner in which the 3rd and the 5th degrees of the melodic scale become rest tones.

The only true rest tone of a scale (harmonic and melodic) is its key-tone. Therefore, if the 3rd and 5th degrees of the melodic scale possess the quality of rest above all the other tones of that scale, they must possess this quality of rest by virtue of being the nearest-related tones to the key-tone of all the tones comprising the melodic scale. Following is the proof that the 3rd and 5th degrees are nearest-related tones to the key-tone.

Assume the tensed string used in finding the least common denominator.

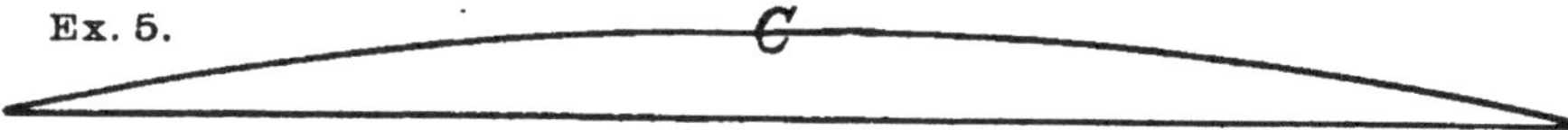


This string vibrates to produce the tone C. In the proof of the least common denominator the tone G was determined as nearest related to the tone C by the division into thirds of the string vibrating C:

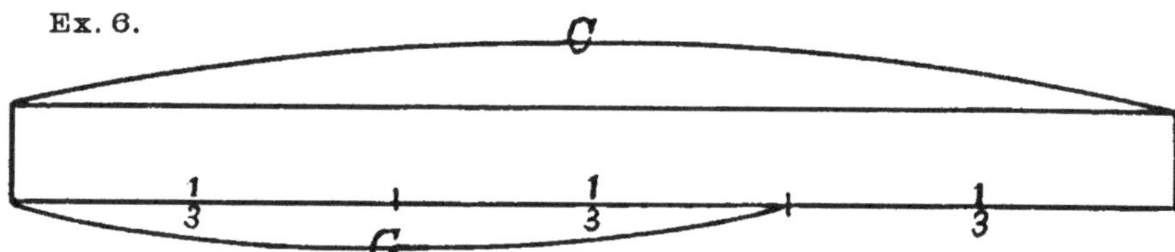


It has therefore already been proved that the tone G is the nearest-related tone to C, thereby establishing in the melodic scale of C the rest quality of the tone G. There still remains the rest quality of the tone E to be proved. The above division of the line shows that the numerical representation of the relationship of G to C is 2 : 3, as the tone G is the result of a $\frac{2}{3}$ division of the original $\frac{3}{3}$ string. What would be the numerical representation for the tone E? Turning to the melodic scale of C it is seen that the tone E is between the tones C and G. Therefore the numerical representation for the tone E would have to be a numeral between 2 and 3. If the equation 2 : 3 is expanded to become as 4 : 6, so as to avoid fractional representation, the tone E will be designated by the numeral 5 and the equation representing the relationship of C, E, and G will become 4 : 5 : 6.

Assume again the tensed string C:

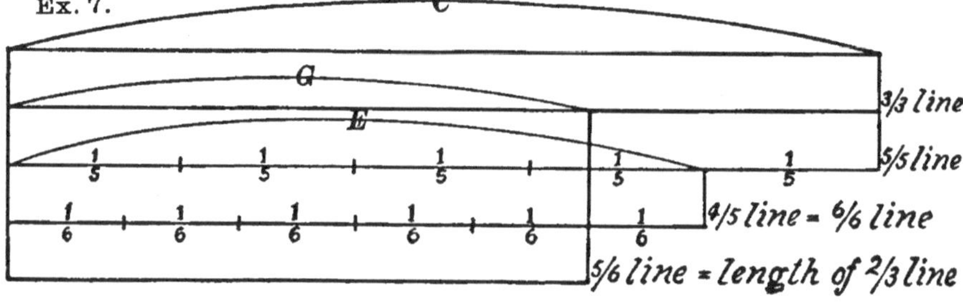

again divide this into 3rds and prove the $\frac{2}{3}$ line as determining G. Assume the same line C, and instead of dividing into thirds, divide this line into fifths and allow $\frac{4}{5}$ of this $\frac{5}{5}$ line to vibrate, and the tone E will result. Assume this $\frac{4}{5}$ line which vibrates E and divide its length into six equal parts and let $\frac{5}{6}$ of that $\frac{6}{6}$ line vibrate and the tone G will result. Therefore $\frac{5}{6}$ of a $\frac{4}{5}$ line is equal a $\frac{2}{3}$ line. It is therefore seen that the tone E is nearest related to the tones C and G because the numerical formula 4 : 5 : 6 represents the simplest relationship in which three tones may stand to one another. Inasmuch as it is a formula which is built upon the simplest relationship of two tones (namely 2 : 3), and also because in proving the tone E as represented by the numeral 5, the tone G is proved as related to E as well as related to C, for it is seen that $\frac{5}{6} \times \frac{4}{5} = \frac{2}{3}$.

E and G, the 3rd and 5th degrees of the melodic scale of C, being the nearest-related tones to the key-tone C, by virtue of this nearest relationship take upon themselves the quality of the key-tone (in the nature of acquired characteristics), and become rest tones in the melodic scale; all the other tones are active tones.

This difference is to be noted between the relationship of active tones in the harmonic scale to the rest tone, and the relationship of the active tones of the melodic scale to the rest tones; in the harmonic scale all the active tones are influenced in their active tendencies by only one rest tone, namely, the key-tone; whereas every active tone in the melodic scale is influenced in its activity by two rest tones, for every active tone of the melodic scale is situated between two rest tones.

Ex. 8.

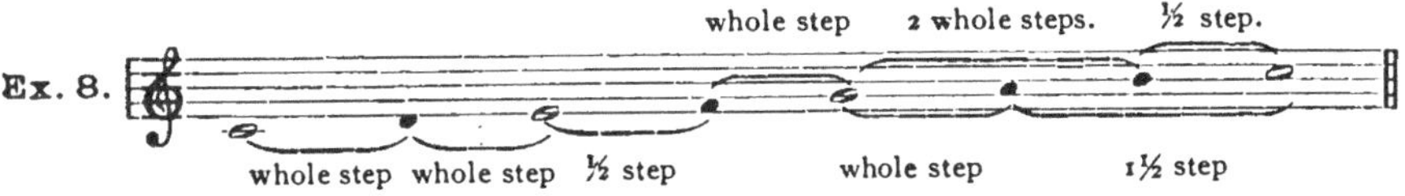


Imagine, in the melodic scale of C, the rest tones C, E and G as magnetic centres; the active tone B, situated between the rest tones C and G, is pulled in two directions at the same time, upward towards C, and downward towards G. But the tone

B is separated from C by a half-step (minor 2nd), whereas the tone B is separated from G by two whole steps; therefore, the active tendency of the tone B is towards the rest tone C, and its quantity of activity is the difference in pull of the rest tone C upon it represented by a half-step and the pull of G upon it represented by two whole steps.

The activity of the tone F, situated between the rest tones E and G, is determined in like manner. The active tone F is separated from the rest tone E by one half-step, and from the rest tone G by a whole step; therefore, the tone F is actively disposed to resolve downward into the tone E, and the quantity of activity that F possesses is the difference in pull of the rest tone E upon it, represented by a half-step, and the pull of G upon it, represented by a whole step. It is thus seen that the active tone F is held back *more* forcefully from proceeding into its point of rest than the tone B is. Therefore, the tone B is more active than F. Similarly, the active tone A is more active than the active tone D, but less active than F. As a result of the above reasoning, the relative activities of the active scale-degrees of the melodic law are as follows:

Most active tone—7th degree of scale = difference between pull of C & G
Next less active tone—4th degree of scale = difference between pull of E & G
Next less active tone—6th degree of scale = difference between pull of G & C
Next less active tone—2nd degree of scale = difference between pull of C & E

Therefore, the melodic law of any scale may be stated as follows (bearing in mind that all the active steps of the melodic law of any key are influenced by two rest tones):

*The direction in resolution and the quantity of activity possessed by any active tone results in the difference in pull in opposite directions of the rest tones affecting the active tone.*

It is therefore seen that the major scale presents two relationships; the first, and most important, is the relationship of all of the tones comprising the scale back to the key-tone. This relationship forms the harmonic scale of the key-tone, — a scale whose tones are separated from each other by perfect fifths; from this relationship is derived the harmonic law of the scale. The activity of the tones of the harmonic law cannot be intuitively felt, as is the case with the active tones of the melodic law; the tones of the harmonic scale will ultimately be found to be root-tones of chords; when the chords which are built upon them are played in relation to the rest chord on the key-tone of the scale, then the varying activities of these root-tones in relation to the key-tone will be felt. It is because of the fact that these tones are roots of chords, that the perfect-fifth scale of any key-tone is called the harmonic scale.

The outcome of the discussion of the laws of the scale should impress upon the mind of the student the realization that all musical phenomena are related through activity and rest; and that music is in reality tonal magnetism. It is the constant seeking of all active musical phenomena for their points of rest, whether those points are the rest tones of the melodic scale, or the key-tone chord of the harmonic scale. If this viewpoint concerning musical phenomena is thoroughly grasped, then the musician will find himself equipped to idealize all fields of human experience, and his musical utterance will have no bounds, for the law which governs the action of tones in music is a universal law; in all probability, this law of activity and rest is accountable for the chemical reaction which happens in a test tube, as well as for the ellipsoidal shape of the earth's orbit. Surely, the human emotions, which are made the subject-matter of musical composition, possess the attributes of quantitative activity as well as qualitative characteristics.

## AURAL PRACTICE

The student should work out all of the diatonic major scales by the foregoing laws of the scale, making each root-tone the point of departure for a series of fifths. After the harmonic scales of the several key-tones are derived, the melodic scales should be formed and the active and rest qualities of the tones noted. The student should also become familiar with the proofs obtained from the subdivision of the tense string, and be able to formulate and discuss these proofs.

# CHAPTER II

## INTERVALS

In Chapter I the laws of the scale were derived and discussed. It was stated that the varying activity of the scale-steps of the harmonic law *could not* be intuitively felt. Furthermore, the varying activity which these harmonic scale-steps possess would become aurally apparent only when chords were erected upon them, and related to the rest chord built upon the key-tone. It was also stated that the varying activities of the melodic law *could* be intuitively felt; therefore it would seem advisable to present first the phenomena which represent the action of melodic law and, in the succeeding chapters, the phenomena which represent the action of the harmonic law.

Intervals are tonal representations of the melodic law. An interval is the relationship which one tone bears to another with regard to pitch. An interval is always named and determined along the diatonic major scale of the lower tone; the numeral name of the upper tone is the numerical name of the interval; if the upper tone of the interval is one of the natural tones of the scale of the lower tone, the interval is said to be diatonic.

Diatonic intervals are of two kinds, perfect and major: The perfect intervals are the unison, fourth, fifth, and octave; these are composed of the key-tone of the scale as the lower tone, and the 1st, 4th, 5th and 8th steps of the scale as the upper tones. In the scale of C the perfect intervals are the following:

Ex. 9.

unison. fourth. fifth. octave.

The major intervals are the second, third, sixth and seventh. These are reckoned from the key-tone of the scale, the upper tone of the interval being the 2nd, 3rd, 6th or 7th of the scale. In the scale of C the major intervals are the following:

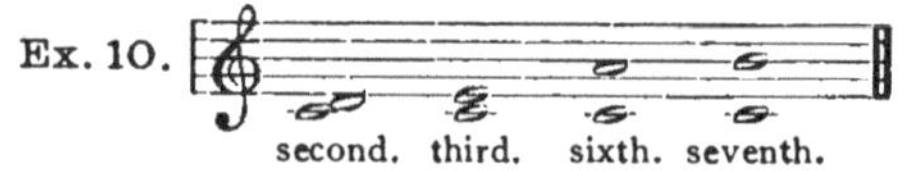

If, however, the upper tone of an interval is not found to be one of the natural degrees of the scale of the lower tone, such an interval is called a chromatic interval. The perfect and major intervals may become chromatic by placing an accidental before the upper tone. By this means the perfect intervals become augmented and diminished; the major intervals become augmented and minor.

If the chromatic sign before the upper tone of the perfect interval *raises* its pitch one half-step, the interval becomes larger by that amount and is said to be augmented. If the chromatic sign before the upper tone of the perfect interval *lowers* its pitch one half-step, the interval becomes smaller by that amount and is said to be diminished. It will be found that perfect fourth intervals may become double augmented intervals by using a chromatic sign that will enlarge the original perfect fourth interval one whole step. It is also possible to lower the pitch of the upper tone of the perfect fifth interval one whole step by use of a chromatic sign, thereby making that interval a double diminished interval. Affixed are examples of the perfect intervals changed to become augmented, diminished, double augmented, and double diminished intervals.

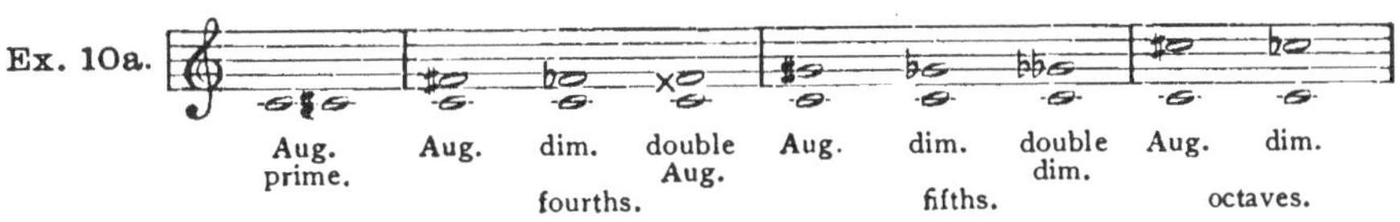


The augmented prime, and augmented and diminished octaves, are less frequently used than the chromatic 4ths and 5ths. The double augmented fourth and the double diminished fifth may result from chromatically lowering the lower tone of the augmented fourth, and chromatically raising the lower tone of the diminished fifth. For example:

It is to be noted in all of the chromatic intervals, that the letter-names of the tones do not change; the original tones are merely changed from diatonic tones to chromatic tones.

The major intervals may also become chromatic intervals by raising or lowering the pitch of the upper tones by means of chromatic signs.

If the upper tones of the major 2nd, 3rd, 6th and 7th are raised one half-step, these major intervals become augmented, for example:

In this series of augmented intervals, the augmented second and augmented sixth are much used. The augmented third and augmented seventh are seldom employed.

If the upper tones of the major intervals are lowered one half-step, these major intervals become *minor* intervals. For example:

All of these minor intervals are used to a great extent. They can undergo further chromatic alteration by lowering the upper tones of which they are composed one half-step, or by raising the lower tones one half-step. For example:

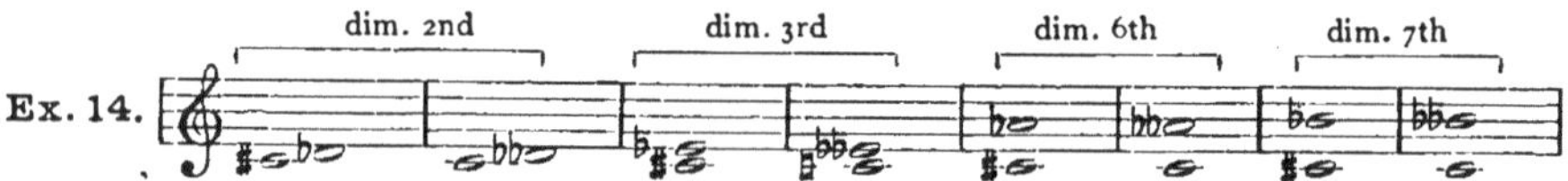


The diminished seconds and sixths are seldom used. The diminished thirds and sevenths are much used.

In naming the diatonic intervals perfect and major, it is inferred that perfect intervals are composed of tones more nearly related to each other than the tones of the major intervals. The proof of the relationship of the tones which form an interval is referred to the natural phenomenon called the chord of nature (also called the overtone series of a fundamental tone).

Let the tone C again be represented by the tense string, and allow that string to vibrate; the string will not only be found to vibrate in its entire length, but will also vibrate in parts, first in halves, then thirds, then fourths, then fifths, etc., and all of these subdivisional vibrations occur in conjunction with the vibration of the full length of string. The tones resulting from these subdivisional vibrations will constitute, with the fundamental as the bass tone, the phenomenon called the chord of nature. This chord of nature built from the root-tone C is illustrated below: The tones resulting from the subdivisional vibrations of the string, are numbered and the relationship of one tone to another is numerically determined by a ratio made from these numerals.

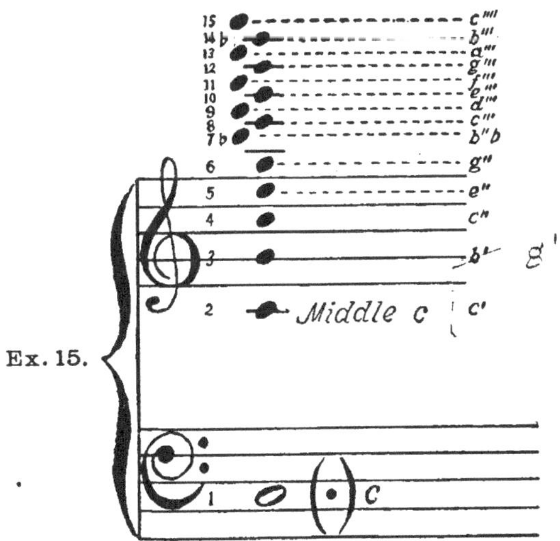


The tone resulting from the vibration of the entire length of the string is represented by the open note (𝅝). The numerical equation representing such a vibrational relationship is 1 : 1; the notes above the root-tone represent the tones resulting from the half, third, fourth, fifth, sixth, seventh, etc., divisions of the string and resound the tones C (1 : 2), G (1 : 3), C (1 : 4), E (1 : 5), G (1 : 6), B♭ (1 : 7), etc. It is seen that the first interval relationship of a tone with the fundamental may be determined as a tone whose pitch is the same as that of the fundamental represented by the note (in brackets, to the right of the open note representing the fundamental). This interval is called a unison or prime. The next interval relationship of a tone with this root-tone is made by the tone Middle C (so-called). This interval is called an octave. The interval formed by the tone above middle C (namely, the tone G) with middle C is a fifth. The interval formed by the tone C above with the tone G is a fourth. It is therefore seen that the first intervals determined by the relationships of the overtones of the fundamental are the perfect unison (1 : 1), perfect octave (1 : 2), perfect fifth (2 : 3) and perfect fourth (3 : 4). They are therefore proved to be intervals formed by tones most intimately related to the fundamental, comprising as a group the first overtones of the fundamental. Because of these significant facts they are called perfect, and are also judged to be consonant, i.e., agreeable to the ear in sound. The degree of consonance, even in the case of the perfect intervals, is discovered, by the ear, as gradually decreasing as the numerical ratios of the tones become more complicated.

The interval formed by the tone e′ above with the tone c′ is a major third, and is represented by the ratio 4 : 5. The interval formed by the tone g′ above with the tone e′ is a minor third and is represented by the ratio 5 : 6. Then occurs another minor third between g′ and b′♭, after which interval there occurs another duplication of the root-tone c, called c″. It is therefore seen that the second set (or class) of intervals determined by the relationship of the overtones of the funda mental are the major 3rd (4 : 5) and the minor 3rd (5 : 6). The reappearing fundamental tone c″ closes the class of major intervals.

## INVERSION OF INTERVALS

The inversion of an interval is effected by reversing the tones of which the interval is made up. In the inversion the lower tone becomes the upper tone; in other words, the lower tone of the interval is placed an octave higher. According to the results arrived at in the first chapter, concerning the octave of a tone, it is seen that the inversion of an interval and the interval itself are practically the same relationship.

To return to the major intervals appearing between c′ and c″, namely, the major third (4 : 5) and the minor third (5 : 6), it is seen that if these intervals are inverted, they result in the minor sixth and the major sixth intervals, which, with the original major and minor thirds, comprise the next class of consonant intervals. The numerical ratios representing these intervals are more complicated than those representing the perfect consonant intervals. They are therefore called imperfect consonances, and become the last consonant intervals determined by the ear.

The attention of the student is called to the recurrence of the pitch of the key-tone c, first by the tone middle C (c′), next by the tone c″, and again by the tone c‴.

The duplication of the root-tone in the successive octaves would seem to determine certain well defined groups into which the intervals so far determined may be found.

The setting apart, in the first group, of the unison and octave establishes an aural experience of the relationship of a tone to itself and makes the ear conscious of the fact that the register (place) of a tone does not affect its pitch.

The setting apart, in the second group between middle C and c″, of the perfect fifth and fourth establishes the aural experience of the limitation of perfect consonant interval relationship. All of the perfect consonant intervals will be found to be hollow and uninteresting in sound; this is due to their perfection in tonal relationship; the more perfect an interval becomes the more difficult it is to hear.

The setting apart in the third group, between c′ and c″, of the imperfect consonances, namely, the major and minor thirds and their inversions, the minor and major sixths, establishes the aural experience of the limitation of the imperfect consonant interval relationships. All of the imperfect consonant intervals will be found to be interesting and significant in sound, thereby making the aural experience of them over against the aural experience of the perfect consonances easy.

The attention of the student is also called to the relationship in sound of all consonant intervals as being one which affects the ear, as a relationship of tones at rest. The consonant intervals when sounded do not seek to move. They sound static; they may therefore be judged as being resultant, and not casual; as static, not dynamic. This fact will be found to be of great importance in the chapters dealing with the structure of triads.

To return to the intervals appearing between c''' and c'''' in the series of overtones: The interval appearing between c''' and d''' is a major second (8 : 9), whose sound no longer affects the ear as a consonance, for the sound-waves which form these two tones are so conflicting as to affect the ear in a disagreeable manner. This interval is, therefore, called a dissonance. The inversion of this interval is the minor seventh (d'' to c''') and is also a dissonance. The other dissonant interval is found to be the minor second between the tone b''' and c'''' (15 : 16), extremely dissonant in character. The inversion of the interval is the major seventh (c'' — b'').

It is therefore discovered that the dissonant intervals are set apart in the fourth group, between c'' and c''', and that their dissonant qualities are represented by complicated or extended numerical ratios (8 : 9 and 15 : 16). The sound of all of the dissonant intervals will be found to be most easily discerned by the ear, for they are all disagreeable to the point of being aurally painful in the case of the major seventh and minor second.

The attention of the student is also called to the relationship in sound of all of the dissonant intervals as being one which affects the ear as a relationship of tones that are active. The dissonant intervals when sounded seek to move. They sound dynamic; they may therefore be judged as being causal, not resultant; as dynamic, not static. This fact will also be found to be of great importance in the chapter dealing with the structure of seventh-chords.

The active dynamic quality of a dissonance demands that the dissonance shall resolve (dissolve) into a consonance, therefore a dissonance is said to resolve; a major dissonance will be found to resolve, by expanding, into a consonance; a minor dissonance will be found to resolve, by contracting, into a consonance. Consonances are found therefore to be possessed of rest qualities. If they move to other consonances they are said to progress, not to resolve, for by their action they do not change their character as consonant intervals. Affixed is a table of the consonant and dissonant intervals.

| | | |
|---|---|---|
| CONSONANCES | Perfect | perfect unisons and octaves |
| | | perfect fifths and fourths |
| | Imperfect | major thirds, and their inversions, minor sixths |
| | | minor thirds, and their inversions, major sixths |
| DISSONANCES | | Major seconds, and their inversions, minor sevenths |
| | | Minor seconds, and their inversions, major sevenths |

## CHROMATIC INTERVALS

All the chromatic intervals should be thought of as changed diatonic intervals, and their classification as consonant or dissonant should be aurally determined. It is recommended that the student aurally determine to which class (consonant or dissonant) the chromatic intervals belong. All augmented intervals will be found to progress or resolve by expanding; all diminished intervals will be found to progress or resolve by contracting.

## AURAL PRACTICE

The aural practice of the chapter on intervals is most important. Intervals should be aurally practiced in two ways:

First, let the intervals be presented melodically, i.e., the tones of which they are composed sounded one after another.

Second, let the intervals be presented harmonically, i.e., the tones of which they are composed sounded simultaneously.

The order of presenting the intervals should be, first, diatonic perfect and imperfect consonances; second, diatonic dissonances. Both of these classes of intervals are to be played as intervals unrelated to any scale. Such interval practice is for the purpose of training the ear to hear untonal intervals, such as occur for example between the tones in the soprano voice, of two keys, in the process of a modulation. The name of the interval is to be determined from its sound; after this exercise of naming the interval has been gone through, the student names the lower tone of the interval and writes the upper tone to correspond to the name of the interval previously determined. When the tones are represented on the staff the intervals are to be sung (the lower tone again being determined).

After the untonal interval practice has been completed the diatonic consonant and dissonant intervals should be practiced as tonal intervals, i.e., practiced in relation to a scale. The student should play the scale and then reinforce the feeling of tonality by sounding the rest tones, 1, 3, 5 and 8. The diatonic, consonant and dissonant intervals are then played and the tones forming the interval within the determined scale are written, and the interval is named from its sound. The tones forming the interval are tones of the melodic law; the interval thus sounded in any melodic scale will be made up of the active and the rest tones of that melodic scale; therefore the intervals should be made to progress or resolve in accordance with qualities of rest or activity which the tones comprising the interval possess. For example, if the interval F to A be played in the scale of C, the interval is first named (a major third). These two tones are now to be auralized[1] as active tones in the scale of C, and the interval then determined as *progressing* to the interval E to G, named a minor third and auralized as composed of rest tones of the scale of C. By this method of presenting intervals the aural experience of the interval as a representation of the melodic law is established.

This form of practice should be applied to intervals in all the fifteen major keys. The tonal practice of intervals should include the playing of the interval in harmonic as well as in melodic form. Examples of melodic tonal intervals and harmonic tonal intervals are shown:

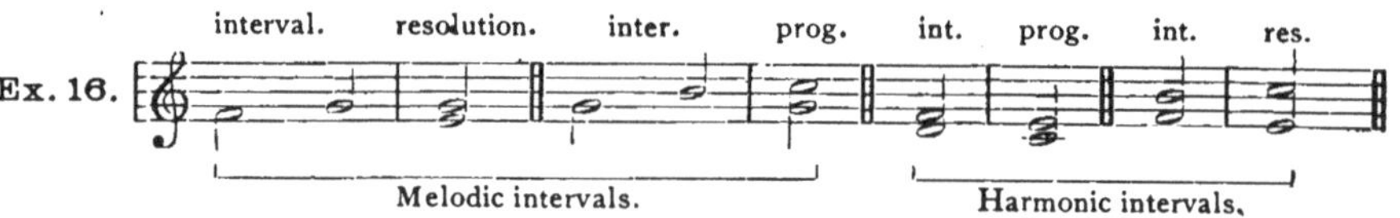


[1] Conceived by the ear; a coined word.

Before auralizing the chromatic intervals the student should make a list of the more commonly used chromatic intervals, and parallel their sounds with the sounds of the diatonic intervals. For example:

The augmented second sounds like the minor third.
The augmented third sounds like the perfect fourth.
The diminished third sounds like the major second.
The diminished fourth sounds like the major third.
The augmented fourth has no diatonic parallel.
The double augmented fourth sounds like the perfect fifth.
The diminished fifth has no diatonic parallel.
The double diminished fifth sounds like the perfect fourth.
The augmented fifth sounds like the minor sixth.
The augmented sixth sounds like the minor seventh.
The diminished seventh sounds like the major sixth.

The chromatic intervals tabulated above are found in the following scale. The scale is called an harmonic chromatic scale. The chromatically altered tones which enter into the formation of this scale become the tones which enter the structure of chromatically altered chords. Using the scale of C as a basis, such a scale is as follows:

Ex. 17. 

The augmented seconds are found between C and D♯, G and A♯, and A♭ and B.

Ex. 18. 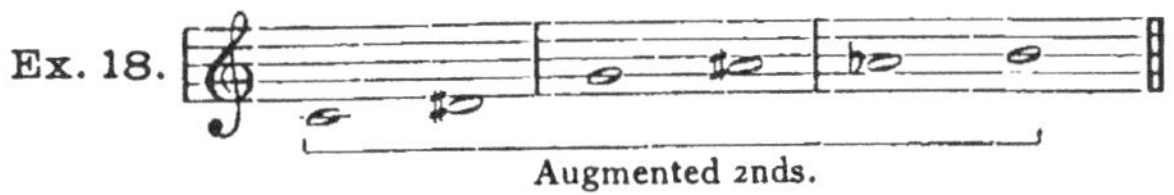


The diminished thirds are found between B below middle C and D♭, and F♯ and A♭:

Ex. 19. 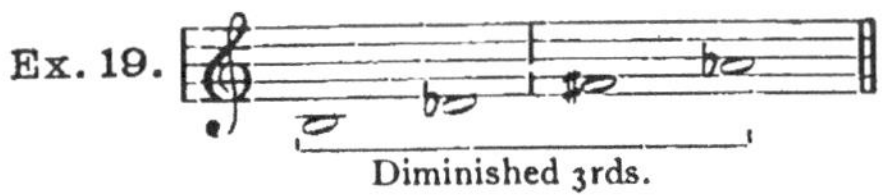


The diminished fourth is found between D♯ and G:

Ex. 20. 

The augmented fourth is found diatonically between F and B, and chromatically between C and F♯, D and G♯, D♭ and G.

Ex. 21.
augmented fourths.

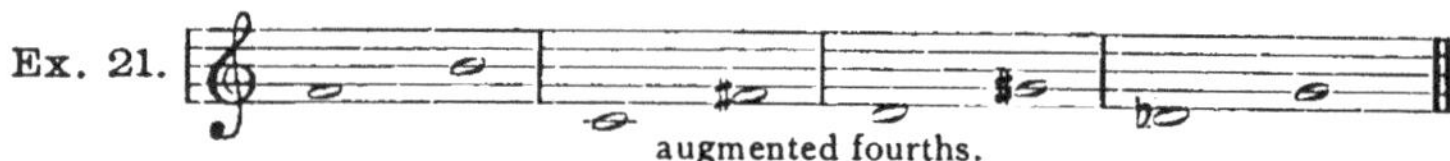

The double augmented fourth is found between A♭ and D♯ (above C):

Ex. 22.
Double augm. fourth.

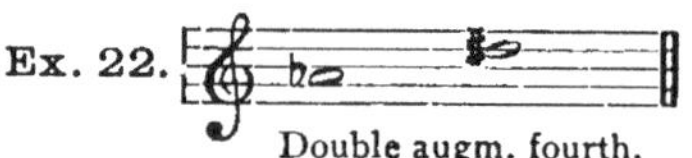

The diminished fifth is found, diatonically, between B (below middle C) and F, and chromatically between D and A♭, C♯ and G, F♯ and C, and G♯ and D (above C):

Ex. 23.
Diminished fifths.

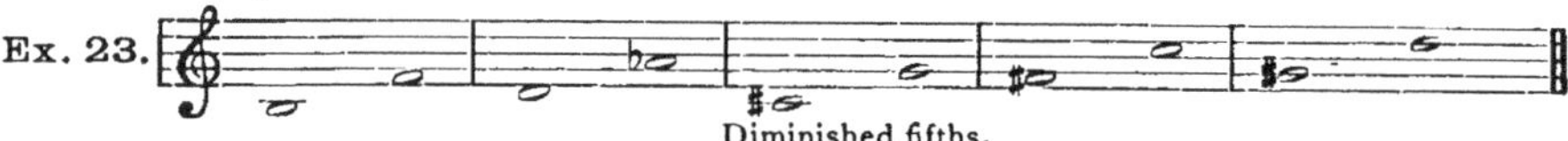

The augmented fifth is found between G and D♯ (above C):

Ex. 24.
Augm. 5th.

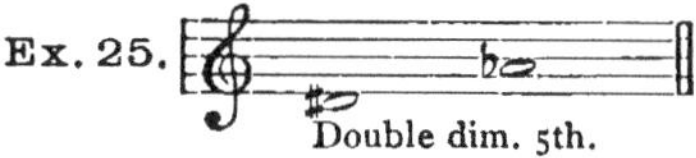

The double diminished fifth is found between D♯ and A♭:

Ex. 25.
Double dim. 5th.

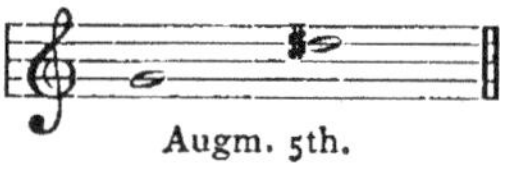

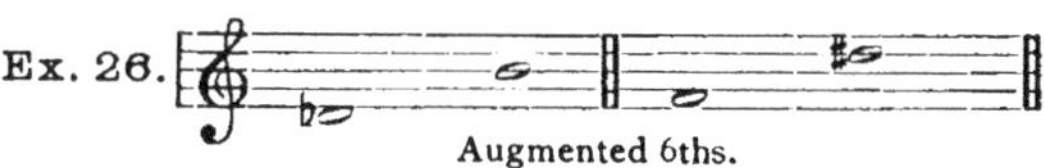

The augmented sixths are found between D♭ and B, F and D♯:

Ex. 26.
Augmented 6ths.

The diminished sevenths are found between B (below middle C) and A♭, D♯ and C:

Ex. 27.
Diminished 7ths.

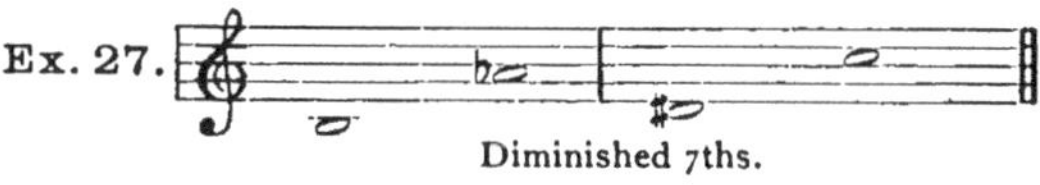

The chromatic intervals illustrated are intervals that will be found as parts of chromatic chords. These should be practiced first. Then the chromatic intervals falling between any chromatic tones of the given harmonic chromatic scale should be practiced. The chromatic intervals should always be given in relation to a scale, else their chromatic quality will not be apparent. For example, a diminished fourth, sounding as it does like a major third, will be auralized as a major third and never a diminished fourth, unless played in some stated key; for it is in relationship to the scale that the activities of the scale-steps will be felt, thereby determining the tones of the interval.

The resolution of all chromatic intervals should always be determined. Most of the tones comprising the chromatic intervals resolve by half-steps into their points of rest. The chromatic intervals employing the ♯ prime, ♯ 5th, and ♯ 6th must be determined by undergoing a double resolution. For example, the diminished fifth between C♯ and G will have to undergo a double resolution, like this:

Ex. 28.

It is readily seen that if such a double resolution for the tone C♯ is not determined, that tone will always sound D♭ (instead of C♯), making the interval an augmented fourth instead of a diminished fifth.

On account of the great number of possible chromatic intervals, and their strange structure, it is thought advisable to make the study of the chromatic intervals first a tonal study and then an untonal study. Many strange chromatic intervals will be found in the soprano voice between unrelated keys, which it would be futile to attempt to tabulate. The intervals of this kind will have to be discussed as they appear. An example of such an interval is cited below.

In the soprano voice of this four-part structure the interval is undoubtedly a double diminished second, the upper tone F flat being (in pitch) lower than the tone E sharp.

It is advised that the diatonic intervals be so thoroughly auralized that the student becomes able to write and sing them;

then the tonal harmonic chromatic intervals should be auralized and sung in like manner. These exercises should be presented in *all* keys. The treble and bass clefs are also to be employed in the writing of intervals.

Accompanying the aural practice of the several kinds of intervals, discussion is to be carried on regarding the emotional quality of the intervals. For example, the purity and simplicity of the perfect consonances in contrast to the varying emotional qualities of the imperfect consonances; minor thirds contrasted with major thirds; the natural sound of the diatonic interval versus the artificial sound of the chromatic interval; and so on. Such discussion is advised in order to prepare the student's mind to discern more fully the emotional qualities of chords, when such discernment is demanded.

A most important method of practicing the interval work of this chapter is to present the intervals as isolated phenomena (i.e., not attached to any scale); the student should auralize the isolated interval, giving first its diatonic name, and then establish the scale to which such a diatonic interval belongs by singing the scale. . After this has been done, the same interval is named the chromatic interval the sound of which is equivalent to the diatonic interval, and the scale to which that chromatic interval belongs is determined by singing. For example, the interval E to G is sounded and named — first — a minor 3rd and the scale of "C" is sung, making the tones of the interval the third and fifth of the scale of "C." The same tones are again struck and the interval is renamed an augmented second and the tones comprising the interval are changed from E–G to E–F double sharp and the scales of E major and G sharp minor are sung. Again the same interval is named an augmented second and the tones comprising the interval are again changed to become F flat–G and the scales of A flat major and minor are sung. This is to be done for all the diatonic intervals whose sounds are analogous to the sounds of chromatic intervals. In this way the chromatic intervals are taught as sounding like the diatonic intervals and the student becomes accustomed to hear the sound of an intricately written interval as soon as he sees the interval. The melodic action of chromatically altered tones is also most forcefully presented through scale singing.

## Intervals to be Practiced Melodically and Harmonically

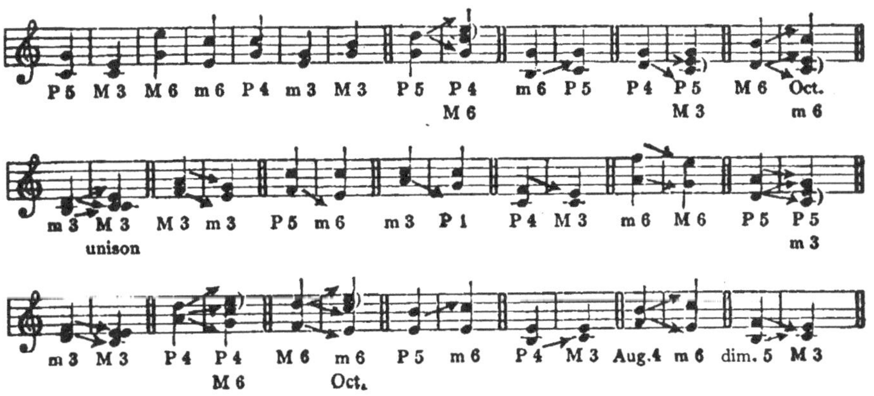


The above diatonic intervals are to be practiced as melodic intervals and as harmonic intervals; the first seven intervals are formed by rest tones, therefore they have no interval of resolution; the other intervals given are formed with their intervals of resolution within the double bars. These intervals should be transposed at the key-board to all keys and their resolutions determined. Each interval and its resolution should be named.

## Chromatic Intervals to be Practiced Melodically and Harmonically

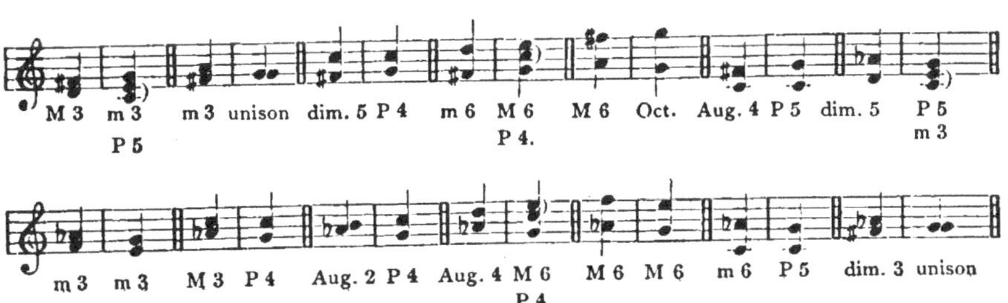

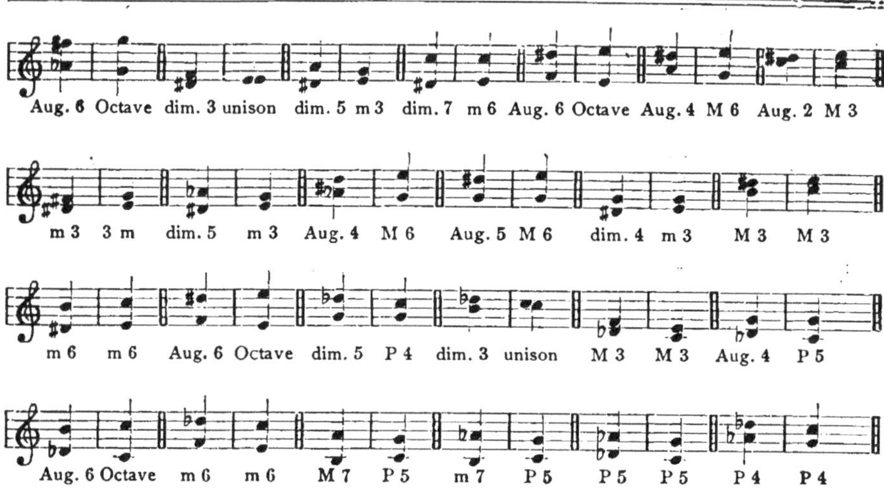


In all of the chromatic intervals, above written, the chromatic tones have single resolution, as represented by the interval of resolution.

The chromatic intervals written above are seen to demand double resolution before the tones of which they are composed resolve to rest tones. All of the chromatic intervals, possessing single and double resolution, are to be transposed to all other keys. Each interval should be named; in the case of the double resolving intervals, the interval of resolution is named from the last tones of the double resolution.

It is also advised, when dictating the intervals above written, to mix the diatonic and chromatic intervals and that the intervals of both classes be chosen at random from the above lists. The intervals of the above lists should also be melodically dictated by playing the upper tone first, in other words, downward.

---

# CHAPTER III

## CHORD-CONSTRUCTION, AND THE TRIAD

A chord is a phenomenon composed of three or four tones of the scale, sounding simultaneously and built up from a root-tone in a succession of thirds. In this phenomenon there is a preponderance of consonant intervals over dissonant intervals.

Two kinds of chords are possible:

1. A three-tone chord called a triad. The intervals forming a triad are all consonant intervals, therefore the chord is called a concord.

2. A four-tone chord, called a seventh-chord, named from the interval relationship formed by the uppermost tone (or last superimposed third) with the chord-root; the chord is therefore called a discord.

The attention of the student is called to the discussion of the chord of nature in Chapter II. It is noted that the overtones of the fundamental which occurs between c and c′ are the first of the series of overtones to arrange themselves in thirds; this arrangement of overtones, in thirds, employs the overtone c″ as a root tone. The triad, determined as a concord, appears first and results from the relationship in thirds of the overtones e″ and g″ with the overtone c″ as the root-tone. The numerical ratio representing such a triad is seen to be 4 : 5 : 6. These numerals therefore must represent tones which are nearest related in pitch to one another; for it is obviously the simplest numerical ratio representing tones in the relationship of thirds. This constitutes another *natural* proof of the fact that the simplest relationship of two tones with the keytone of any scale determines those tones as rest tones in the melodic law. (Chapter I, page 9.)

The seventh-chord, determined as a discord, appears next in the chord of nature, and results from the relationship in thirds of the overtones E, G and B flat, with the overtone C as a root-tone; it is noted that the interval of a seventh which enters this chord-structure is a minor seventh, therefore the structure of seventh-chords is determined as including only the dissonant interval of a minor seventh.

After the appearance of the seventh-chord structure in the chord of nature the next overtone which appears is another duplication of the fundamental, namely, the overtone c‴. Therefore it is to be deduced, that, as in the case of the classification of intervals, so in the case of the chord-structures the reappearance of the fundamental as an overtone closes the class of chords which are employed in establishing the laws of the scale of which they are a part.

### THE TRIAD

A chord called a triad is composed of a root, a third above the root, and a fifth above the root. The triad is therefore a concord, being composed entirely of consonant intervals. Therefore, concords are limited to three-tone structures, the triads alone comprising this class of chords. It has been cited in Chapter I, in the discussion of the harmonic law, that the tones of the harmonic scale are employed as roots of chords. The other two tones which enter the structure of the triad, are tones of the melodic law. The triads upon the harmonic degrees of the scale of C are as follows:

In the above illustration the root-tones are written as open notes, the melodic tones as closed notes, to indicate (visually) their difference in character. It is also seen that the order in which the triads follow one another is the order of their root activities. The I triad is the key-tone triad and is the rest chord. The most active triad is the triad on the fifth degree, called the V triad, or dominant triad, because of its intense impulse to progress harmonically into the rest triad, I. The II triad is the next less active triad. The IV triad is the next less active triad. The relation of these triads to each other, to affirm the key, is determined by the harmonic activity of the root of the triad.

Any triad may progress harmonically to a triad whose root is more active than its own. Therefore the V triad has but one possible harmonic progression, namely, into the rest triad I. The II triad may progress harmonically into the V triad or directly into the I triad. The IV triad may progress harmonically either into the II triad, the V triad, or the I triad. It is also apparent that the V triad cannot progress harmonically into the IV triad, for in so doing the V triad would be harmonically progressing against the law which governs the activity of its root. Such a progression of the V triad annuls the tonal consciousness of the key and is called a deceptive progression.

Referring again to the triads erected upon the root-tones of the harmonic scale, it is noted that all of them possess within their structures the interval of a *perfect* fifth with their roots, excepting the triad on the seventh degree, whose fifth forms an interval of a diminished fifth with its root. When a triad's fifth is perfect, the triad is named from the character of its third. Therefore, the I triad is found to be major, because the interval from C to E is a major third. The V triad is also major, because the interval from G to B is major (determined along the scale of G). The II triad is minor, because the interval from D to F is a minor third (measured along the scale of D). The IV triad is major, its third, F to A (measured along the scale of F), being major. The VI triad is minor, its third, A to C (measured along the scale of A), being minor. The III triad is also minor, as its third (measured along the scale of E) is minor. The VII triad is diminished, for its fifth is found to differ from the fifths of all the other triads (whose fifths are perfect); therefore, the triad takes its name from its fifth, and is called a diminished triad.

The triads of a key establish, by their interrelationship, the laws of the key; they are also made up of the tones of the harmonic and melodic scales. Thus they are servants of the key.

Triads are further designated as primary and secondary. A primary triad of any key is a triad whose character agrees with the character of the key to which it belongs. Therefore the major triads, I, V and IV, are primary triads. The minor triads II, VI, III, and the diminished triad VII, are secondary triads. It naturally follows that the primary character of triads should be sustained and not lessened, while the secondary character of triads should be minimized, lessened.

Triads are employed in writing four-voice structure, analogous to the choral structure. Therefore it is necessary to find another tone in the triad to furnish this fourth voice. One of the tones of the triad is doubled to obtain this fourth voice.

In the process of doubling one of the triad's tones, the triad is affected by the preponderance of the sound of the doubled tone, and the result upon the ear is to intimate in the triad the sound of the triad built upon that doubled tone as a root. In short, *any tone which is doubled in a triad intimates the triad built upon that doubled tone.*

It is therefore seen that a triad may be affected in two ways, as a result of doubling in its structure the different tones of which it is composed. The two ways in which any triad may be affected by doubling one of its tones to find a fourth voice, are,

First, its individuality may be changed;

Second, its character, as well as its individuality, may be changed.

For example, take the primary triad on the first degree (the I triad) in the key of C major. The triad is composed of the tones C, E, G. First, double in this triad the root-tone C, and it is seen that the triad, by virtue of the doubled tone, more fully emphasizes its own self, or is reinforced in sounding its own individuality. Second, double in this I triad the fifth, G. According to the above rule, that the doubled tone of any triad intimates the triad of the doubled tone, the I triad will be made to intimate in its sound not only itself, but also the triad on the tone G. Therefore the I triad has suffered the loss of some of its own individuality in being made to sound the V triad as well as the I triad.

Third, double in the I triad its third, E. The triad on E is a minor triad; therefore, by intimating a minor triad in the I triad by doubling the tone "E," the major quality which that chord possesses has been lessened, and the chord sounds less major than the primary triad on the I degree should sound. Thus the chord has been uncharacterized, and has suffered as a result of the doubled third. It also has lost some of its individuality in sounding the III triad as well as the I triad.

Remember that the triads of a key seek to serve the key by representing its character through their own. The primary triads would have that tone doubled in them, which tends to preserve their character and sound their identity as well; and, therefore, the best tone to double in them is their *root*. If, however, it is desired to intimate in their structure the succeeding triad, and that triad is the triad whose root is the fifth of the original triad, then it is better to double the fifth. In so doing, the coming triad is foreshadowed. Never double their thirds, for in so doing the character of the primary triads is minimized, and the triad will not establish, by means of its sound, the character of the key of which it is a servant.

Turning to the secondary triads of the key, it is apparent that the character of these triads is antagonistic to the character of the key of which they are servants. Therefore it is cxpedient, in doubling the tones of which they are composed, to endeavor to lessen the antagonistic quality that they possess.

In the key of C take, for example, the secondary triad on D, the II triad (D, F, A); if the third of this triad, namely F, is doubled, the triad is made to suggest the triad on F, which triad is a major triad. Therefore the minor character of the II triad is lessened, and the triad is made more adaptable for use in a major key. The same results would obtain in doubling the third of the secondary triads on the sixth and third degrees.

Hence, in the secondary triads in a major key, try to double their thirds in preference to any other tone. Next, double their roots. In voice-leading between triads, it will often be impossible to double the thirds of the secondary triads, but it is advisable to do this whenever possible. The triad on the seventh degree is found in music to be used in but one position, and inasmuch as the subject of inversion has not yet been dealt with, the discussion about the doubling of one of its tones to procure a fourth voice will be relegated to the chapter devoted to the discussion of the triads in minor.

The next step to discuss, in preparing to use the triads, is the four-part, or choral, structure referred to above. A choral structure is divided into four parts (or voices), soprano, alto, tenor and bass. Each of these voices has a definite range. The soprano and alto voices are always written upon the treble staff, the tenor and bass voices upon the bass staff. The range, or register, of the four voices is illustrated below:

Ex. 31.

The best register for the voices is determined as lying between the pitches represented by the half-notes.

A choral structure is written in close or open harmony. Close harmony places three voices, soprano, alto, and tenor, on the treble staff. This form of writing will not be used. Writing in open harmony places the soprano and alto parts on the treble staff and the tenor and bass parts on the bass staff.

In distributing the triad's tones among the four voices, it is required that neither of the three upper voices, namely, the soprano, alto and tenor, shall be separated from an adjacent voice by an interval greater than an octave. So arrange the alto voice that it is not separated from the soprano part or from the tenor part by an interval greater than an octave. The law which governs these three upper voices (soprano, alto, tenor) is the melodic law. This law is established through the medium of activity and rest, within the confines of an octave. Therefore, the voices which represent this law should not be separated from each other by an interval greater than an octave. It is also advisable not to allow the parts to cross, i.e., the alto to become higher in pitch than the soprano.

The bass, when the root of the triad, is always a tone of the harmonic law, and being thus governed by a different law from that governing the three upper voices, it may optionally be separated from the tenor voice by more than an octave.

The soprano part may be given any tone of the triad. If the soprano is assigned the double root-tone of the triad, the triad is said to be in root-position or octave-position. If the soprano is assigned the third of the triad, the triad is said to be in the position of the third. Likewise, if the soprano part is assigned the fifth of the triad, the triad is said to be in the position of the fifth. It must be noted that when in the I triad the soprano is assigned the root of the triad, then only is the triad determined as being entirely at rest. When the soprano is assigned the third or the fifth, the triad will be determined as being active within its own structure. This aural experience is due to the fact that when the outer tones of the triad are the root-tones (first, the root itself assigned to the bass, and second, the doubled root assigned to the soprano), the sound of the triad is as if it were enveloped (or bounded) by its root feeling; but when the soprano is assigned any tone of the triad other than the doubled root, the triad sounds as if one or two tones were outside the boundary of the root, resulting in an active structural sounding chord.

## AURAL PRACTICE

The aural practice essential to this chapter consists, first, in building up all the triads from the several degrees of the scale, noting their major, minor and diminished qualities. This is to be done with the triads as a three-voice structure. This exercise should be practiced aurally until the different qualities of the triads are fully and accurately known. Second, the triads should be arranged by the student in all possible positions that the register of the several voices will permit. For example, the I triad in the key of C as follows:

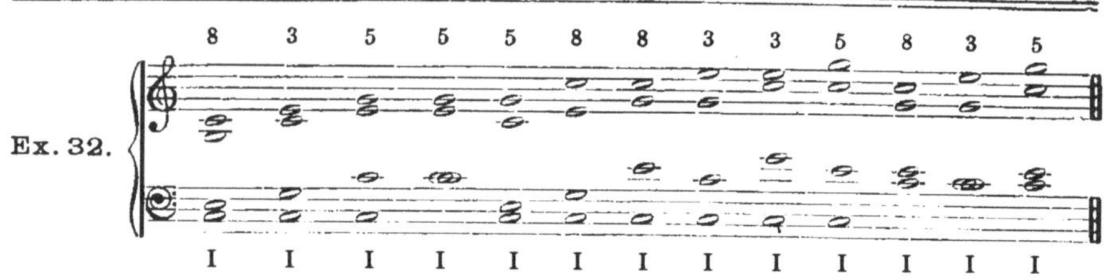


In the preparation of an exercise of this kind, care should be taken to double the root of the triad. The register of the voices should not exceed their limits. Do not cross the voices. Keep the soprano and alto parts on the treble staff, the tenor and bass parts on the bass staff. Arrange the three upper voices of the triad in such a manner as to procure an interval of less than an octave between the alto and the adjacent voices (soprano and tenor). The position of the soprano should be determined in each case by the use of a numeral above the treble staff, and each triad should have the root-tone in the bass voice. Prepare the exercise away from the piano, and then have the exercise played, the student writing the triad as it sounds, attending to the position of the soprano part, and the register of the voices, particularly of the bass and soprano. Lastly, write the triad in open position; first, with its root doubled; second, with its fifth doubled; third, with its third doubled; and note the changes in the sound of the triad's individuality, and character:

Example A. The I triad, by virtue of the doubled root, sounds itself and its individuality is reinforced.

Example B. The I triad, by virtue of the doubled fifth, intimates the sound of the V triad in its structure.

Example C. The I triad, by virtue of the doubled third, is unmajorized, and its character is undermined.

The above exercise should be worked out for the primary

triads of all keys, and then for the secondary minor triads of all keys. It is best for the student to have such exercises played, so that he shall be physically independent of the keyboard. In all of the aural exercises note the structural active qualities in each triad, due to the assignment to the soprano part of the third or the fifth of the triad.

In auralizing the subject-matter of the chapter, the student's attention is called to the fact that by doubling any tone of a triad but its root, the triad is structurally activized. There are two ways in which any triad is made structurally active:

First, by assigning to the soprano a tone of the triad other than its root;

Second, by doubling in the triad the third or fifth of the triad, to obtain a fourth voice.

## CHAPTER IV

### THE USE OF THE PRIMARY TRIADS IN FOUR-PART WRITING

A triad in which the root-tone is assigned to the bass voice is said to be in its fundamental position. A triad may be brought into two other positions which will be considered in succeeding chapters. In this chapter the primary triads, I, V, and IV, will be used in their fundamental positions. In order to determine the manner in which the harmonic and melodic laws govern the action of the primary triads (as well as of all chords) let us consider the V triad, harmonically progressing to the I triad:

Ex. 34.

Observe that both of the primary triads are written in the fundamental position (roots in the bass), and that the fourth voice in each triad is the tone which doubles its root. In the harmonic progression of the V triad (which is determined by the triad's progressing *over* a bar line), the tone G in the soprano part remains stationary. The tone D in the alto part progresses upward to the tone E in the I triad. The tone B in the tenor part progresses upward to the tone C, while the tone G in the bass part acts, in progressing, differently from any of the upper parts, inasmuch as it leaps to the tone C of the I triad. It therefore naturally follows, that the root-tone progressing by a leap must be governed in its action by a specific law. This law is the harmonic law. It therefore follows that the bass part, when assigned the root of the triad (thereby bringing the triad in the fundamental position), is a tone of the harmonic law, and acts in accordance with its dictates. The three upper voices are found to act diatonically, and by virtue of their diatonic action it is determined that they are all tones of the melodic law and governed in their action by that law. They are therefore grouped together, and should always be brought into such proximity with one another that they, by their relationship to one another, determine the law which governs them. It is to be noted that all progressions of the active tones of the melodic law, seeking their points of rest, occur within the confines of an octave. Therefore, it is found expedient not to separate the middle voice of the three upper voices, namely, the alto, from either soprano or tenor by an interval greater than an octave. The bass of the V triad leaps the interval of a perfect fifth in its progression to the bass of the I triad. This leap of a perfect fifth is the interval which separates the fifth step of the harmonic law from the key-tone. Therefore, this bass tone, being the root of the triad, is a tone of the harmonic law and acts in accordance with the dictates of that law.

It follows, that a triad in the fundamental position (as, in fact, any chord) is composed to two kinds of tones;

(1) An harmonic tone, the bass, and

(2) Three melodic tones, the soprano, alto and tenor.

It will also appear that the melodic tones, in their action, are dependent upon the action of the harmonic bass tone. This would naturally follow, for it has already been shown that the melodic law is derived from the harmonic law, and is, therefore, dependent upon it.

The example illustrated the case of the most active triad, V, progressing harmonically into the rest triad, I. This is the only *harmonic* progression which the V triad can make, because of the position of its root in the harmonic law in relation to the key-centre.

Let us now take the example of the IV triad progressing harmonically into the I triad:

Here the triads are in their fundamental positions, with their root-tones doubled, and the laws which govern the relationship of the chords are described as occurring over the bar line. The three upper parts of the IV triad are seen to progress diatonically; this determines that they are governed by the melodic law. They are also grouped together, being less than an octave apart in their adjacent interval relationship. The bass voice of the IV triad, the root of the triad, leaps in progressing, thereby affirming the fact that it is governed by the harmonic law.

The harmonic progressions of the primary triads to the rest triad, which have been represented and described, are very important. The first one, namely of the V triad to the I, is obviously the harmonic progression of the most active triad to the rest triad (for the root of the V triad is the nearest tone of the harmonic law to the key-centre). The harmonic progression of the IV triad to the I is not so important, for the root of the IV triad is further away from the key-centre than the root of the V triad. Therefore, the harmonic progression of IV into I will affect the ear as less impetuous, less virile, less active, than the harmonic progression of V into I. This is the manner in which the ear discerns a difference between the V triad and the IV triad. In sound they are alike, for they are both major triads; but they differ in harmonic activity.

When any active triad harmonically progresses to the rest triad (I triad), a *full effect* of the key is said to occur. When a full effect of a key occurs, it is apparent that all active tones of both the harmonic and melodic laws seek their points of rest.

When, however, any active triad harmonically progresses to an active triad which is nearer the key-centre, thereby setting up the consciousness of the harmonic law, a *semi-effect* of the key is said to occur. In such use of an active triad, the active tones of the triad which belong to the melodic law (namely the upper voices) may or may not seek their points of rest, for the progressing triad has not sought to establish the harmonic law through full effect, but through semi-effect. This is shown below, in the case of the IV triad harmonically progressing to the V triad. It is obvious, in such a progression, that the action of the root of the IV triad establishes the harmonic law, for it is in harmonic progression towards a tone of the harmonic law (namely, the root of the V triad), which is greater in activity than itself; but in such a progression the active tones of either law, with the exception of one tone, do not progress to their points of rest, and still the feeling of the key is determined by the pronouncement of the harmonic law through the action of the root-tone of the IV triad.

Ex. 36.

As in the previous examples, these triads are shown in the fundamental position with their roots doubled to procure a fourth voice, and the harmonic progression of the one to the other occurs over the bar line. It would seem in the above example as if the bass voice progressed diatonically (i.e., stepwise) upward. If this progression *were* a diatonic progression upward, and thus an action in the melodic law, the activity of the fourth step would be contrary to the dictates of the melodic law, which determines that the fourth step shall progress *downward*. This misuse of a tone of the melodic law would affect the musical ear to the point of calling such a use of the fourth step unnatural and unmusical. But this root-tone of the IV triad, placed in the bass, is a tone of the harmonic law and not of the melodic law, and its progression, seemingly diatonic and upward, into the root of the V triad, is in reality a leap downward, passing through (or by) the II tone into the V tone in its journey towards the key-centre (I tone).

Ex. 37. IV V I

This instance is a strong proof of the fact that the bass tone of a chord, when the root of the chord, is a tone of the harmonic law and not a tone of the melodic law. It is the greatest of fallacies to represent a chord as being erected upon the steps of any melodic scale. The chord should always be represented as being erected upon the tones of the harmonic scale.

The three upper voices of Example 36 are acting melodically, although only one active tone, namely, the soprano, A, progresses to its point of rest, G. The active tone in the alto voice is progressing through its point of rest to the active tone D of the V triad. The rest tone C seemingly relinquishes its rest quality, and progresses to the active tone B of the V triad. It would seem, therefore, that the melodic law had been set aside for the moment. But this is not the case; the fact that is being forcefully determined in this example is that the melodic law in its action waits for the dictates of the harmonic law, and is subservient to the harmonic law. In other words, the tones of the melodic law which are used as the three upper tones in of any active chord are able to assert their active tendencies, and thus resolve to their points of rest, only when the chord of which they are a part harmonically progresses to the I triad, that is, produces a full effect by its harmonic progression.

Semi-effect in the key is also established by the action of the I triad harmonically progressing into either the V triad or the IV. Affixed are the examples of these harmonic progressions:

It is to be noted in both examples that the melodic rest tones remain at rest where it is possible (in the tenor voice of both examples), and it is further noted that the bass voices (roots of chords), being harmonic in character, leap in progressing.

These examples, with the others previously presented and explained, illustrate how the primary triads may be harmonically related among themselves. Tabulated, the results are as follows:

Full Effects { V triad to I triad
IV triad to I triad

Semi-Effects { IV triad to V triad
I triad to V triad
I triad to IV triad

It is apparent that the case of the V triad harmonically progressing into the IV triad is impossible. Such a semi-effect would not affirm the harmonic law by the action of the V triad, for in the case of such an harmonic progression, the active root of the V triad would be harmonically progressing into the *less* active root of the IV triad, thereby nullifying the harmonic law of the key. Such a relationship of the primary triad would deceive the ear in the consciousness of the feeling of the key-centre. The progression is, therefore, prohibited.

From the above examples certain facts (or rules) may be deduced:

First, chords which are related to one another by the harmonic and melodic laws are represented as preceding and following a bar line. The bar line is therefore a sign of law. In the chapter on Metre it will be shown that in simple metre the position of the bar line determines the place where the laws of the key are established. In compound metre each measure will contain an harmonic relationship of chords which will not be established by the presence of the bar line, but will be aurally discerned as occurring through the feeling of grouping of chords within the measures as those measures are used to form a phrase length.

Second, when a chord is in the fundamental position, the bass tone is harmonic in character and progresses by leaps.

Third, the three upper voices, being melodic in character, should proceed, as often as possible, by stepwise progression.

Fourth, the skip of a third in the progression of any upper voice is not considered a leap.

Fifth, certain parallel perfect fifth intervals, and all parallel perfect octave and unison intervals, are to be avoided. An interval has been defined as a representation of the melodic law. The perfect unisons, octaves and fifths, in parallel action, are considered able to destroy the consciousness of the law of which they are representations. For this reason they are held to be bad.

The melodic law is written (or framed) to determine a relationship existing between two tones in music through the medium of activity and rest. In order to determine a relationship there must be a difference. In the case of the perfect intervals, one of the interval's tones must be an active tone, the other a rest tone. If such a difference is present in the make-up of a perfect interval, there is undoubtedly a relationship of the melodic law determined by the sound of the interval. It is obvious that in the case of perfect unisons and octaves both tones forming the interval must be of the same character, either rest or active tones, but in the case of the perfect fifth it may happen that such an interval is made up of one active and one rest tone.

Ex. 39.

For example: note the illustration in the key of C. The first fifth is made up of an active tone and a rest tone. This is also true in the case of the second interval. Therefore, both of the perfect fifth intervals establish, within their own structure, a relationship of the melodic law by possessing in their structures different kinds of tones (namely, active and rest tones), and it is impossible to see how by their parallel action the melodic law can be broken down. If, however, a perfect fifth interval, both of whose tones are rest tones or active tones, progresses in parallel action to another perfect fifth interval, both of whose tones are rest tones, or active tones, it is admitted that such a parallel progression may contradict the melodic law and therefore may be considered bad. An example of such a progression in the key of C is here given:

Ex. 40. 

Again, if one of the perfect fifth intervals is composed of an active and a rest tone, while the other perfect fifth interval (into which it progresses in parallel motion) is not composed of different kinds of tones, such a succession is judged to be good. Any relationship in tone must be judged as good or bad according to whether it affirms or contradicts the law which it represents. Therefore, the *sound* of an interval-progression is not the fact which determines whether that progression is good or bad. Furthermore, the interval of a fifth in the chord ensemble is the least discernable interval in the strueture; for the more perfect an interval is, the more difficult it is to hear. It may be omitted in the chord-structure (as will be seen in the case of the dominant seventh-chord), without affecting the structural accuracy of the chord's sound; being therefore the negligible interval it cannot, when used in parallel successions, be contended against as sounding badly, because such parallel successions of perfect fifths are seldom, if ever, heard.

### AURAL PRACTICE

The aural practice of the chapter should be as follows: Establish the key feeling by playing the scale of the key. Sound the I triad of the key (always in four-part, open, harmony) by playing the soprano and alto parts in the right hand, tenor and bass in the left. Do this employing the V triad, and then the IV triad. Note that all the triads sound major; write the chords in all soprano positions and register and auralize the characteristic sounds resulting from the different arrangements of the parts of the triad. For example (for the I triad, refer to previous chapter), the V triad in the key of C:

Example B would rarely occur, being outside the compass of the tenor voice. In example E the three upper parts should be played by the right hand.

Construct a similar example for the IV triad. Do this in as many keys as possible, writing out the I, V and IV triads in the several keys, at the keyboard; at first away from the keyboard, endeavoring to hear the effect of the triad as written.

The next exercise is to combine the active primary triads, V and IV, with the rest triad I, in all possible combinations within the compass of the several voices, thereby setting up the key by full effect.

The harmonic progression of the V triad into the I, when it occurs as the last harmonic effect of a phrase, is called an Authentic Cadence.

All rules for triad-building and part-leading should be carefully adhered to.

The example of the IV triad progressing harmonically to the I triad, when it occurs as the last harmonic effect of the phrase, is called the Plagal Cadence.

The next exercise consists in combining the triads so as to set up the key by semi-effect.

First, the IV triad progressing harmonically to the V triad.

Second, the I triad progressing harmonically to the V triad.

Third, the I triad progressing harmonically to the IV triad.

In this example note the incompleteness of key feeling. Be sure that the key-centre is kept in mind by periodically playing the I triad.

The same incompleteness of key feeling results in examples 2 and 3; in a less degree, however, due to the presence of the I triad in all the harmonic progressions of both exercises. These Exercises 1, 2 and 3 should be played in many keys.

## CHAPTER V

### THE PHRASE AS DETERMINED BY THE HARMONIC RELATIONSHIP OF THE PRIMARY TRIADS IN THEIR FUNDAMENTAL POSITIONS

A phrase in music corresponds to a sentence in speech. It is the simplest unit of all musical form. It is generally composed of four measures, but it may be two measures (small phrase), or eight measures (large phrase), in length. Phrases of two, four or eight measures are called regular phrases. Irregular phrases are those of three, five, seven, etc., measures. A phrase ends in a chord-relationship called a cadence.

Cadences are determined as points of posture which result from the harmonic relationship of chords, and they determine for the ear the end of the phrase. The Cadence that most effectively determines such a point of posture is produced by the V triad harmonically progressing to a I triad. Such a V to I cadence is called a perfect cadence. It is noted from the illustrations in the previous chapter that all chord-relationships occur over bar lines; therefore, the perfect cadence requires that the I triad shall occur on the strong pulse of the penultimate measure of the phrase whose limit in length it determines; the V triad which harmonically progresses into the I triad is placed on the last pulse of the preceding measure. The strong pulse is the pulse upon which a triad of resolution is placed. The weak pulse is the pulse upon which a triad which is harmonically progressing is placed. The accentuated or strong pulse which is aurally felt in successive places in the length of a phrase is the place where a triad has harmonically progressed into a triad of resolution. It is therefore apparent that pulses are grouped as a result of harmonic progression, and are said to be weak or strong according as they become pulses upon which triads harmonically progressing are placed or pulses upon which triads of resolution are placed. The grouping of strong and weak pulses is visualized by the bar line. The portion of a phrase between two bar lines is called a measure.

Therefore, the phrase is spoken of as a four-, two- or eight-measure phrase.

Let the foregoing explanations be illustrated by a four-measure phrase. In all of the measures comprising the length of this phrase there are placed triads of resolution and triads harmonically progressing:

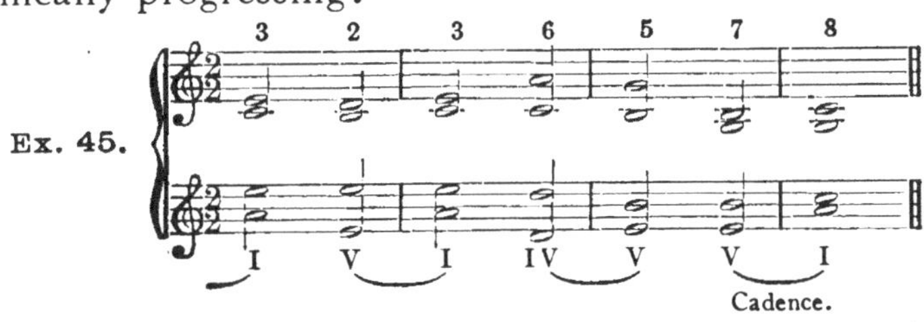


The phrase is seen to begin with the I triad placed on the first pulse of the first measure. The phrase also ends with a perfect cadence formed by the V triad harmonically progressing into the I triad. · The length of the phrase is determined by the sum of the harmonic progressions which occur within it. The I triad on the first pulse of the first measure has no triad harmonically progressing into it. It is, however, implied that this triad is a triad of resolution, inasmuch as it succeeds a bar line. The pulse upon which this triad occurs is therefore judged to be a strong pulse. The I triad on the first pulse of the second measure is determined as a triad of resolution, being the triad into which the V triad, preceding the bar line, harmonically progresses. The V triad on the first pulse of the third measure becomes the triad of resolution of the harmonically progressing IV triad, and the phrase ends with the perfect cadence previously explained. Therefore, within the phrase-length there are four pulses upon which triads of resolution occur, and the phrase is therefore spoken of as a four-measure phrase.

Again assume a four-measure phrase, in each measure of which there are three triads instead of two:

The triads which are harmonically related are the triads preceding and succeeding the bar lines. The phrase begins on the strong pulse. The IV triad on the first pulse of the second measure is the triad of resolution of the harmonically progressing I triad, preceding the bar line. The V triad on the first pulse of the third measure is the triad of resolution of the harmonically progressing IV triad preceding the bar line, and the phrase again ends in the perfect cadence formed by the V triad harmonically progressing over the bar line into the I triad. Therefore, this phrase (as in the case of the first example) is determined as a four-measure phrase. It is, however, to be noted that each measure of this phrase contains three triads, and but two of the three triads are related to each other as triads harmonically progressing and triads of resolution. The triad on the second pulse of each measure is an unrelated triad and is not connected with the triad on the first pulse, or with the triad on the third pulse, by law. These triads on the second pulses of each measure are therefore unrelated triads, i.e., they do not become triads of resolution, or triads harmonically progressing; for this reason any succession of triads may occur within the confines of a three metre measure. The important triad of each measure is therefore the harmonically progressing triad, and this triad must in its harmonic progressions over the bar line set up the harmonic law of the kev to which it belongs.

To illustrate, assume again the triads of the key of C major:

Ex. 47.

In example A the IV triad preceding the bar line follows the V triad, and harmonically progresses over the bar line into the I triad. In so doing it establishes the harmonic law of the key by its progression into the I triad. The harmonic law of the key is in no way affected by the fact that this IV triad follows the V triad, which triad is placed upon the second pulse in the confines of the measure, for the triads upon the second and third pulses are not harmonically related by law. If, however, as in example B, the IV triad becomes the triad of resolution, by becoming the triad upon the first pulse of the second measure, and the V triad is determined as harmonically progressing into the IV triad, then the harmonic law of the key will not have been established, for the active triad V has but one harmonic progression, namely, into the I triad; and by harmonically progressing into the IV triad it acts against the dictates of the harmonic law by harmonically progressing away from the key-centre, instead of toward it. This harmonic progression of the V triad is therefore not allowed. The above citations clearly represent the difference between the harmonic progression of a triad and the non-harmonic progression of a triad. The harmonic progression of a triad establishes the harmonic law of a key. Non-harmonic progression of a triad does not determine (or undetermine) harmonic law.

In Example 45 at the beginning of this chapter the phrase is said to be in two metre. In Example 46 the phrase is said to be in three metre. Metre is the arrangement of pulses within the confines of a measure. Metre is of two kinds, duple and triple. In duple metre all of the pulses are harmonically related. In triple metre, the second pulse in each measure is an unrelated pulse. It is therefore apparent that the harmonically progressing triads in both kinds of metre must establish the harmonic law of the key of which they are servants, by their harmonic progressions over the bar lines. The bar line therefore determines visually the place where the two triads are related by law. The bar line would seem to separate visually the triads on either side of it, rather than relate them to each other, but this visual paradox is easily overcome by regarding the bar line as the sign of junction between two chords related to each other by the harmonic law of the key of which they are servants.

In using the primary triads to form duple and triple metre phrases, the student must conform to the rules cited in the previous chapter. These rules determine the action of the voices of a triad which harmonically progress over the bar line (as is seen in the examples given). The progression of the voices between triads which are merely progressing from one to the other within the confines of a measure are not governed by rules or laws, and a freer use of the voices is possible. The inner voices (alto and tenor) may leap in such a progression, but the faulty parallel interval-progressions (perfect parallel unisons, octaves and fifths) must be avoided.

It was shown in the previous chapter that the inner voices of an harmonically progressing triad must proceed over the bar line diatonically (that is, stepwise), for it was determined that these inner voices of the triad are melodic in character. Therefore, if they leap over the bar line, the law which governs them is not affirmed. The result of such faulty leaping of the inner voices is to produce accent upon the pulse succeeding the bar line (for where a law is broken in music, the ear is shocked), which pulse is already determined as an accented pulse by virtue of becoming the pulse upon which the triad of resolution is placed. Two accents would then be present upon this first pulse of the measure, and the *legato*, or smoothness, of the phrase-structure would suffer. Therefore, such voice-leaping is not considered good.

## ACCENTS

There are two structural accents in music;

First, the accent resulting from the harmonic progression or resolution of a chord;

Second, the accent resulting from the leaping of the inner voices of a chord as it harmonically progresses or resolves into the chord of resolution. Both accents should not be present at the same time, for in that case the *legato* of the phrase is disturbed.

If a chord is repeated over the bar line, the ear is not conscious of the harmonic progression, or resolution, of the chord. In this case, the inner voices may leap; but if the chord preceding the bar line harmonically progresses or resolves into another chord, thereby affecting the ear as an harmonic progression or resolution, the inner voices must progress diatonically.

In passing it may be stated that dynamic accent (tonal quantity) is dramatic accent, and is never structural in character, nor does its employment affect the metre of a phrase. Dynamic accent is used to heighten the emotional utterance of a phrase whose structural length has already been determined.

As a result of the reasoning outlined in this chapter, it is imperative always to present chords in relation to one another, so that they by virtue of that relation establish a phrase-length. It is further seen that the chord relationships which establish the phrase-length will so group themselves within the measures of that phrase as to establish the metre (either duple or triple) in which the phrase is written.

## AURAL PRACTICE

The aural practice of this chapter is important, and should proceed in the following manner:

The student should firmly establish the feeling of tonality by playing the I triad of the key and by causing the V triad to progress harmonically into the I triad. He should then play the phrase which is to be auralized, and determine the metre in which the phrase is written. The triads which by their relationships to each other have determined the phrase-length, and the metre, are then indicated below the bass staff, by the use of Roman numerals, as the I, V or IV triads. The Roman numeral is therefore the symbol of the harmonic law. It is made to represent the triad in its entirety. Two playings of the phrase for the symbolizing of the harmonic law are advised. The student is then to symbolize the melodic law as it is represented by the tones of the soprano voice. The symbol used to represent the melodic law is the Arabic numeral, placed above the treble staff. In symbolizing the melodic law the active or rest qualities of the tones of the soprano part are the facts to be taken account of. Do not count up or down from any known scale-step to determine another scale-step, but auralize the tone as either restful or active in quality, and determine what tone of the scale it is by its relationship in the melodic law of the scale. After the symbols of both laws have been written, the student should again play through the phrase and write the notes of the soprano part, thereby representing the registers and the metric values of that given voice.

It is apparent that the two selective features of any exercise which are at the disposal of the instructor are

First, the chord-relationships and progressions,

Second, the melody of the soprano. Both of these selective features must conform to the laws which govern them. They are therefore symbolized:

(1) The more important one, namely, the harmonic progression of triads;

(2) The melodic progression of the soprano. The notes of the soprano are written merely to determine the register (place) and time-value of the tones which are selected for that voice.

The outer voices (soprano and bass) of the triads are thereby determined, and the inner voices are then added, in accordance with the rules already established in the previous chapter. The primary triads in their fundamental positions are used to establish the phrase. Duple and triple metre phrases are employed, and the exercises are written in all keys.

After the exercises are auralized and written, the student should play them, noting the active and rest qualities of the chords. The student should then employ the practice material to develop the retentive power of his mind, by playing the phrase through once, and memorizing the chords and melody. If such a task be found too difficult at first, the student should play the phrase, first writing the numerals and notes for the melodic law, and then writing the Roman numerals which are the harmonic symbols of the chords. The student should memorize triad succession in these simple metres in groups over the bar line. Always hear and memorize triads in relationship, and not as a succession of isolated chords. The phrase thus auralized should then be transposed to all other keys in keyboard work.

Phrases employing the I, V and IV triads should be improvised at the keyboard, and retained by the student as they are afterwards written and played. In such improvisational work at the keyboard the student should be alert to detect faulty voice-progressions, due to leaps of inner parts, and faulty parallel perfect interval progressions.

8 2 3 4 2 7 8
I V I IV V V I
5 5 5 6 5 7 8
I V I IV V V I
3 6 5 5 6 5 5
I IV V I IV V I
8 6 5 2 3 2 1
I IV V V I V I
3 5 6 5 5 5 5
I I IV V I V I
3 2 3 4 2 7 8
I V I IV V V I
8 5 6 4 2 7 8
I I IV IV V V I
3 4 3 5 6 5 5
I IV I I IV V I
5 6 5 7 8 7 8
I IV V V I V I
3 1 1 7 8 2 1
I I IV V I V I
5 3 2 4 3 2 1
I I V IV I V I
8 7 8 5 6 5 5
I V I I IV V I

8 8 7 2 3 2 1 8 5 6 4 2 7 8
I IV V V I V I I I IV IV V V I
1 2 3 5 6 5 5 8 7 8 3 4 2 1
I V I I IV V I I V I I IV V I
3 5 5 6 5 7 8 5 6 5 1 2 5 5
I I V IV V V I I IV I I V V I
8 2 3 1 7 2 1 3 2 3 5 6 5 5
I V I I V V I I V I I IV V I
3 2 3 4 3 5 6 5 7 8 8 8 6 5 3 4 3 2 5 5
I V I IV I I IV V V I I IV IV I I IV I V V I
5 6 5 5 3 2 3 4 2 3 8 5 5 5 6 4 3 2 5 5
I IV V I I V I IV V I I I V I IV IV I V V I

3 4 2 3 5 6 5 2 7 8
3 2 4 3 5 6 5 3 2 3
I IV V I I IV V V V I
I V IV I I IV I I V I
8 2 3 4 3 6 5 2 5 5
8 5 3 4 6 5 5 3 2 1
I V I IV I IV V V V I
I I I IV IV V I I V I
3 5 6 5 5 3 4 2 5 5
1 2 3 4 6 5 5 2 7 8
I I IV V I I IV V V I
I V I IV IV I V V V I
5 6 8 7 2 3 4 2 5 5
1 2 5 5 3 4 3 2 7 8
I IV IV V V I IV V V I
I V V I I IV I V V I
3 2 4 3 2 3 4 2 7 8
8 5 6 5 3 2 3 6 5 5
I V IV I V I IV V V I
I I IV I I V I IV V I
1 2 4 3 1 1 7 1 2 1
5 8 7 8 3 4 3 2 7 8
I V IV I I IV V I V I
I I V I I IV I V V I

3 5 6 5 2 3 4 2 7 1
I I IV V V I IV V V I
5 6 5 5 8 2 3 4 2 1
I IV V I I V I IV V I
5 5 6 5 3 4 2 5 7 8
I V IV I I IV V V V I
3 4 2 3 5 6 5 3 2 3
I IV V I I IV I I V I
8 5 6 5 2 3 4 3 2 1
I I IV V V I IV I V I
5 6 4 3 2 3 4 2 5 5
I IV IV I V I IV V V I
3 2 5 5 6 4 3 4 2 3
I V V I IV IV I IV V I
5 4 2 3 5 6 5 2 5 5
I IV V I I IV V V V I
8 5 4 3 2 3 4 6 5 5
I I IV I V I IV IV V I
3 4 2 3 5 6 5 3 2 3
I IV V I I IV I I V I
3 5 5 5 6 4 3 2 7 8
I I V I IV IV I V V I
5 6 5 5 3 1 1 7 2 1
I IV V I I I IV V V I

---

# CHAPTER VI

## MELODY — HARMONIZATION OF MELODIES

A melody is a series of single tones sounding consecutively. A melody must possess five characteristics, namely· Intervals, Tonality, Metre, Rhythm, and Proportion.

The intervals made by the difference in pitch between the successive tones must be composed of tones in a definite scale. They must arrange themselves in groups, which become measures of a phrase. In these groups, composed of two, three or more pulses, there must be a recurrence of the accented and weak pulses, which recurrence is called rhythm. Finally, the succession of groups or measures forms, in summation, a larger group or unit called the phrase, which larger group, when contrasted with another phrase (made up in the same manner as the first phrase), determines the last characteristic of melody, called proportion.

The subjects of intervals and of tonality have been discussed. The subject of metre has been touched upon, but not fully discussed.

A phrase is said to be in two or in three metre. A phrase is also spoken of as in simple or compound metre. The first use of the term metre determines the number of pulses (or beats) in a measure. If the measures of which a phrase is composed contain two pulses, the phrase is said to be in two metre. If a phrase is made up of measures, each containing three pulses, it is said to be a three metre phrase.

In every two metre phrase, each pulse within the measures is one of two kinds, namely, a pulse upon which a chord of resolution occurs, or a pulse upon which a chord harmonically progressing (or resolving) occurs. The bar line is the visual representation of the pulses that are thus connected. Therefore, in two metre the second pulse within the measure is the pulse upon which the harmonically progressing (or resolving) chord is placed. The first pulse within the second measure is the pulse upon which the chord of resolution occurs. For example:

In the above example the IV triad is the harmonically progressing chord, and is placed on the second pulse of the first measure. The I triad placed upon the first pulse of the second measure is the chord of resolution. By virtue of being determined as the chord of resolution of the harmonically progressing IV triad, the I triad of the second measure becomes accented. Therefore, in two metre, the first pulse of each measure is the accented pulse. The second pulse is the unaccented pulse.

In three metre, as in two metre, the first pulse is accented, being the pulse upon which the triad of resolution is placed. The third pulse is the unaccented pulse, being the pulse upon which the harmonically progressing triad is placed. It has been previously established that the second pulse of each three metre measure is unattached to either the first or third pulse. Upon this second pulse may be placed any triad, no matter what triad precedes or succeeds it, for such a triad would be unrelated harmonically to either the preceding or the succeeding triad. The second pulse in three metre is therefore considered an unaccented pulse.

In example A the V triad, on the third pulse in the first measure, progresses harmonically into the I triad on the first pulse of the second measure. The IV triad on the second pulse is unattached either to the I triad preceding or to the V triad succeeding. In example B the V triad, on the second pulse, is the unattached chord, for if it were attached to the succeeding triad as an harmonically progressing triad, such a relationship would break down the harmonic law of the key. This, however, is not the case, therefore the V triad and IV triad are not harmonically related to each other.

In the above examples of two and three metre, the triads on the first pulses of the first measures of each example are accented, although there are no triads represented as harmonically progressing into the triads of resolution. A phrase which begins in this manner, namely, on the accented pulse, is said to begin on the *thesis*, and the incomplete effect resulting from starting on the *thesis* is called by some theorists an incomplete figure, by others an incomplete motif. It is readily seen that these figures, or motifs, are the smallest division of the phrase, and when summed up they determine its length in simple metre.

When a phrase begins on the unaccented pulse, the first figure, or motif, is found to be complete. Such a phrase is said to begin on the *arsis*.

In simple metre, the pulses of each measure can be related to each other only in one way, namely, as resolving and resolution pulses.

In compound metre, the pulses of each measure can be related to each other in two ways:

First, as resolving and resolution pulses, and

Second, as pulses grouped together, to form resolving and resolution groups. For example:

Ex. 51.

In the above example, starting on the thesis, the I triad on the first pulse is an incomplete figure (or motif). The IV triad on the second pulse progresses harmonically into the V triad on the third pulse, thereby determining the third pulse as an accented pulse. The V triad on the fourth pulse progresses harmonically over the bar line into the I triad, determining the pulse as an accented pulse. It is therefore seen for the first time that an accented pulse may occur within the confines of a measure. This is always the fact in compound metre, and is one of the aural signs of *compound* metre as contrasted with *simple* metre.

The chords in the first measure of the example may be made to form groups: the first and second pulse chords form the first group; the third and fourth pulse chords form the second group. The last group, formed by the third and fourth pulse chords, may be made as a unit to resolve over the bar line into the group formed by the first and second pulse chords of the second measure. Such grouping is shown by the illustration of an entire phrase, rather than any shorter length, for compound metre over against simple metre is only determined as existing by the relationship of chords within a phrase-length. The above results may also be illustrated in the following manner, permitting each chord to be represented merely as a pulse:

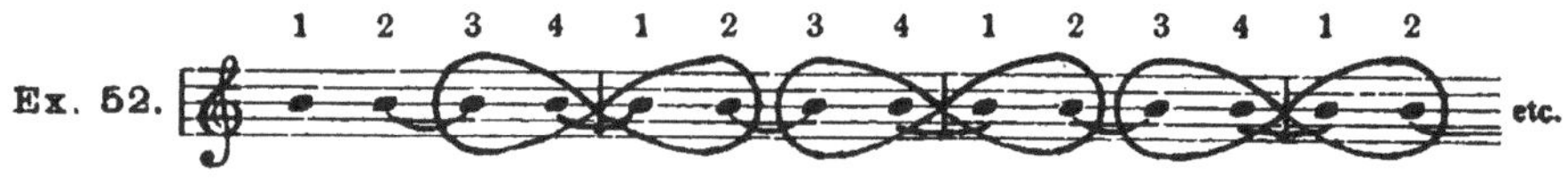


The harmonic relationship of the pulses to one another is illustrated by the brackets joining such pulses, second pulse with third pulse, fourth pulse with first pulse of succeeding measure. This relationship determines the first pulse and third pulse of each measure as accented pulses.

The group relationship of the pulses to one another is illustrated by the circles including the grouped pulses. It is seen that grouped pulses always resolve over the bar line, thereby accenting the first pulse of each measure.

As the result of the above outline the first pulse of each measure of compound metre is found to possess two accents,

First, an harmonic accent and

Second, group accent.

The third pulse of each measure possesses but one accent, an harmonic accent. This accounts for the feeling of strong and less strong pulses in compound metre of all kinds.

If in the phrase of compound metre, illustrated above, the harmonic accent is maximized and the group accent is minimized, the metre signature employed will be represented by the symbol $\frac{4}{4}$:

If, however, the group accent is maximized and the harmonic accent is minimized, the metre signature employed will be an incomplete circle with a line through it 𝄵 (called allabreve four metre):

If the phrase is played to determine the harmonic accent, four pulses are given for each measure; if it is played to determine group accent, two pulses are given for each measure. It is seen that allabreve four metre differs from $\frac{2}{2}$ metre, although each is determined by beating two pulses to the measure, in that allabreve four metre is more *legato* than $\frac{2}{2}$ metre. In allabreve four metre, the second pulse in each measure is still harmonically related to the third pulse, although not taken account of in the manner of beating the measure, whereas in simple $\frac{2}{2}$ metre the first and second pulses are never related.

In writing melodies in phrase-form to given harmonies, the simple two and three metres are first employed; then the more complicated compound four, six, nine and twelve metres.

Rhythm, determined as the next factor of melody, is said to be regular or irregular. The term rhythm employed in this manner has reference to the recurrence in each measure of the accented pulses in their right positions (or places). It has been noted in the discussion of metre that the accented pulses in simple metre are always the first pulses of each measure. A melody, so written as to effect the ear as having the first pulse in each measure an accented pulse, is said to be in regular rhythm.

Examples of regular rhythm follow:

Ex. 54. 

If, however, by subdivision of the pulses within the measure, the accented first pulse becomes the subdivided pulse, and the unaccented second pulse is undivided, the accent of the measure would aurally seem to occur on the second, rather than on the first pulse. Such a melody is said to be in irregular rhythm.

Examples of irregular rhythm:

Ex. 55. 

Regular rhythm will therefore result from subdividing the unaccented pulses, and allowing the accented pulses to remain undivided. Irregular rhythm will result from subdividing the accented pulses and thereby aurally shifting the accent to the undivided unaccented pulse. It will also be found that the repetition of a chord over the bar line does not aurally determine an harmonic progression as occurring. A repetition will also give rise to irregular rhythm. In writing melodies to given harmonies forming a phrase, regular rhythm should be adhered to for the present.

The last factor of melody, namely, proportion, has to do with the balance in length of the first phrase, as related to the second phrase. This factor will be taken up for discussion when the period is presented. At present the student should write melodic phrases. He is, therefore, not concerned with the proportional arrangement of melodic material.

In writing a melody from given primary triads, certain rules must be borne in mind:

First, the melody should contain but seven tones of the scale at present, and all of these melodic tones will be parts of the primary triads.

The 1st, 3rd, and 5th steps are parts of the I triad.

The 5th, 7th and 2nd steps are parts of the V triad.

The 4th, 6th and 8th steps are parts of the IV triad.

It is seen from the above table that the 1st and 5th steps belong to two triads. The choice of the triads having been made, the melodic tones will readily arrange themselves in accordance with the given triads.

Second, in selecting the melodic tones, there should be no unsingable intervals (such as a major 7th up or down). There should be present, in each melody, *rhythmic* variety, governed in its use by the laws determining regular rhythm. The small rhythmic figures should occur on the same relative pulse in succeeding measures and spring from different scale-steps. This will establish in the melody the structure called sequence, and such a use will annul the rigid ruling of leaps.

Good rhythmic variety is included without destroying the sense of recurring accent.

Ex. 53.

Third, a wider leap than a third in either direction necessitates the change of direction of the succeeding melodic tones. This rule is excepted in the use of sequence. It is also excepted in the use of successive melodic tones which follow a definite chord-line.

A B

Ex. 59.

After leaps of sixths in melody the directions change; as in Example A. In Example B, the successive leaps spell the I triad and are permitted.

Fourth, all the active melodic tendencies outlined in Chapter I should be adhered to. Any diatonic succession, including three or more successive steps of the scale, will set aside the direction of melodic progression of any active tone. In this diatonic use the seventh step may be made to progress downward, the fourth step upward, etc.

All the active steps are progressing in the right direction.

After the student has written melodies to the given harmonies of the exercises of the last chapter, the task should be reversed, and the melody written first. In performing the task, all of the rules for chord-relationship in two and three metre must be respected, the successive melodic tones forming such a melody being so arranged as to admit of their application.

### THE TRITONUS

In the third example illustrating bad leaps, the leap in the third measure, from F to B, is called a tritonus. It occurs in every major key, between the fourth and seventh degrees of the scale. It is an augmented fourth interval, and embraces three whole steps in the same direction (hence its name tritonus). It is considered a bad melodic progression, because the tones of which it is composed are seen to be the most active melodic tones of the scale. These tones demand melodic resolution in different directions; therefore, when they follow one another, one of the two tones will remain unresolved, producing upon the ear an unsatisfactory effect. The tritonus is also found to be unsingable when occurring in either inner voice of a four-part structure. If it is ever indulged in, the progression from 7 down to 4 is better than from 4 up to 7. The progression 4 to 7 may occur when the seventh step is below the fourth.

Ex. 61.

The exercises at the end of Chapter V are to be used as harmonic bases for the formation of melodies according to the rules and laws explained in this chapter.

---

## CHAPTER VII

### THE SECONDARY TRIADS IN MAJOR

The student is required to review thoroughly Chapter III (on chord-structure) before beginning the study of the secondary triads in major. The paragraphs relating to the doubling of the voices in secondary triads are most important.

The harmonic importance of a triad in the key depends upon the approximation of its root to the key-tone of the scale. Referring to the II triad, Chapter I, it will be found that the root of the secondary triad on the second degree is nearer the key-tone than the roots of any of the other secondary triads (in fact its root is nearer to the key-tone than the root of the primary triad on the fourth degree). The II triad is therefore the most important of all the secondary triads.

The II triad may progress harmonically into either the V triad or the I triad. Its harmonic progression into the I triad is stronger and more confirming of the key than that of the IV triad.

The third of the II triad (as in the case of all secondary triads) is doubled; the third of the triad should appear in the soprano voice whenever possible.

Following are illustrations of the harmonic progressions of the II triad:

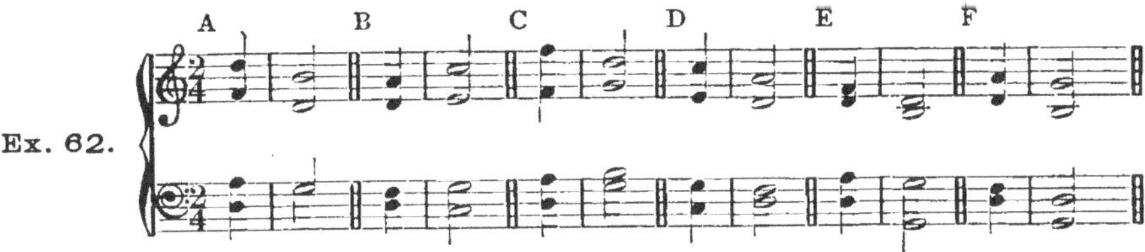

Ex. 62.

In all the above examples, with the exception of Example C, the root of the II triad is doubled. This is made necessary because of the part leading into the triad of resolution, and will occur most frequently when both triads are in the fundamental position.

In auralizing the II triad it must be made to sound like the IV triad, and yet become harmonically more important than the IV triad. The II triad should be made to sound in relation to the V triad, because of the perfect fifth relationship of its root to the root of the V triad, as naturally progressing harmonically into the V triad. The activity of all the triads, with the one exception of the V triad, is not intuitively felt by the ear, therefore the relation of the II triad, through the V triad to the I triad, must be intensely practiced; and after the ear has repeatedly experienced such a relationship, that relationship will ultimately become intuitively felt. The II triad may become the triad of resolution of the IV triad, but it cannot harmonically progress into the IV triad.

The harmonic progression of the II triad into the IV triad is an anticlimax in tonal feeling; such an harmonic progression of the II triad must *at least* be considered as *deceptive;* such use of harmonic material is not advised at present. A law must first be known and understood before it is broken.

Ex. 63.

Example *A* is good because of the correct harmonic progression of the IV triad. Example *B* is not advised, because the root of the II triad progresses harmonically away from the key-centre, that is, into the harmonic tone IV, thereby contradicting the harmonic law, and producing aurally the feeling of anticlimax in the consciousness of the key. Example *C* determines the relationship existing between the IV, II and V triads.

The emotional quality of the II triad must be contrasted with the emotional qualities of the primary triads. It consists in the lack of agreement with the character of the key and gives rise to a hard, crass, unyielding sound, over against the soft, insinuating, yielding, pliable sound of the primary triads. In this way the II triad seems negative, and not positive. It seems to challenge the key instead of representing it. The II triad is a concord, therefore possesses no virility or potency. It may be contended, and correctly, that the II triad is cadentially stronger than the IV triad, but it is to be borne in mind that in using it as a cadential effect, the contrasted qualities of the minor II triad and the major I triad in forming a cadence for a major key do great violence to the affirmation of the quality of the key.

### VI TRIAD

This secondary triad is more remote from the key-centre than any triad previously discussed. It progresses harmonically either into the primarv IV triad, into the secondary II triad, into the primary V triad, or directly into the I triad.

The best tone to double in the VI triad to procure a fourth part is the third; next, its root. If its third is doubled, the triad will intimate the I triad in its sound, and it can therefore be said to be the representative of the I triad. Illustration of the harmonic progressions of the VI triad follows:

The harmonic progression of the VI triad into the IV triad is good. The harmonic progression of the VI triad into the II triad is less good, because of the combining of two minor triads to establish a major key: In writing in major keys the primary subject-matter — namely, the I, IV and V triads — should predominate. Therefore, do not indulge too freely in such harmonic progressions as VI to II. The harmonic progression of the VI triad into the V is good. It is also good to employ the VI triad before the authentic cadence V to I.

The harmonic progression of the VI triad into the I is weak, and should be avoided. The harmonic progression of the I triad into the VI is good. The VI triad combined with the I is best used in adjacent relationship to the I triad, and not in harmonic relationship. For example:

In the above examples the VI and I triads merely stand adjacent to one another and are not harmonically related over the bar line.

### III TRIAD

The secondary III triad is still more remote from the key-centre than any of the triads previously discussed, and because of this fact its harmonic progression is restricted.

The more uncertain and indefinite the harmonic relationship of a chord becomes, the more imperative it is to cause such a chord to progress harmonically according to the successive steps of the harmonic law.

Therefore, the III triad may be made to progress harmonically into the VI triad only. When the III triad is used as progressing harmonically into the IV triad, it resembles a passing-chord in aural effect, and does not sound like a triad structure. For example:

Ex. 67.

The harmonic progression of the III triad into the VI triad is permitted, but not recommended, for both triads are so remote from the key-centre that the effect closely approaches that of a modulation (Example *A*). The harmonic progression of the III triad into the IV triad impresses the ear as a passing-tone effect instead of an harmonic effect. The upper (soprano) voice in both examples, *B* and *C*, progresses diatonically. The bass voice in Example *B* really impresses the ear as written in Example *C*, and the inner voices remain stationary. This fact further accentuates the passing character rather than the harmonic character of the III triad.

The discussion of the VII triad in major will be taken up when the minor mode is reached. It will then be shown that a triad of the same diminished character as the VII triad in major is found on the important second degree in minor. (See the beginning of Chapter XV; also the end of same Chapter.)

## AURAL PRACTICE

The auralization of the secondary triads in conjunction with the primary triads, already experienced, should always be so presented as to bring out the primary and secondary characters of the triads first. The student should determine

First, whether the triad is major or minor in character, and

Second, the harmonic activity of the triad.

From the foregoing discussion it is apparent that these minor triads are of varying importance and value, and this point must be dwelt upon continuously.

The treatment of the varying importance of these minor triads among themselves, and in relation to the major triads, should be approached through the use of the harmonic scale of the key in which the dictation exercise is given. For example: the harmonic law is written

Ex. 68.

for the key used, and the root-tones are then rehearsed in their several possible resolutions in the direction of the arrow. These may be tabulated, and the two triads then played and written over bar lines, in order to auralize and visualize the results of the reasoning as to their possible harmonic progressions.

Following are exercises in two and three metre, including, first, the II triad only, and then the VI and III triads.

In these two-metre exercises the student is required to numeralize the soprano and then the triads in groups of twos, as they successively determine the length of the phrase by the relationships over the bar line. The first phrase is retained alone, and then the second phrase.

The student's attention is called to the cadential effect, closing the phrases.

A cadence may be defined as a rhythmical point of rest, or posture, ending a phrase. Such points of rest fall upon accented pulses and the cadence-chord should be written in note-values of longer duration than any of the chords of resolution upon the strong pulses within the confines of the phrase.

Cadences are described as full or semi-, as perfect or imperfect, and as complete or incomplete.

A full cadence occurs when the cadence-chord (chord of resolution) is the rest triad I.

A semi-cadence occurs when the cadence-chord (chord of resolution) is an active triad. A semi-cadence is formed in two ways.

First, by any active triad harmonically progressing into a triad of greater activity.

Second, by the rest triad I harmonically progressing into any active triad.

A perfect cadence occurs when the V triad harmonically progresses into the rest triad, I.

An imperfect cadence occurs when any active triad other than the V triad harmonically progresses into the rest triad, I.

A complete cadence occurs when the rest triad I is the cadence-chord and appears in the soprano position of the eighth, uninverted, and its root doubled to procure the fourth voice of its structure. In other words, a complete cadence occurs when the rest triad, I, appears as the cadence-chord and possesses all of its structural rest qualities.

An incomplete cadence occurs when the rest triad, I, is the cadence-chord and is made structurally active by being brought in the soprano position of the third or fifth, by being inverted, or by doubling any tone other than its root to procure a fourth voice.

Cadences are named according as they possess one or many of the above characteristics; for example, a cadence may be

Full, perfect, and complete;
Full, imperfect, and complete;
Full, perfect, and incomplete;
Full, imperfect, and incomplete;

and so on.

The mental effort in the retentive (or memory) work should be to grasp the phrase as a unit, and not as a length composed of a succession of chords. This is accomplished by training the ear to become susceptible to full and semi-effect in the key as the triads relate themselves to each other. If the student is unable to retain the triads in groups of twos as they establish the length of the phrase, he may play the phrase through once to establish over each bar line the full or semi-effects which are selected to comprise the phrase-length, and symbolize their effects by the use of the letters *S* (semi-effect) and *F* (full effect), placing the letters at the bar line where the effect occurs. After this has been done, a second playing of the phrase should result in memorizing the triads that make up the several effects symbolized. For example.

In the above illustration, the first effect is a full effect (though not quite complete, owing to the fact that the example begins on the thesis); the second, a full effect (V to I); the third, a semi-effect (II to V); the cadence-effect is full (IV to I). These effects are marked by the letters *F* and *S* at the first playing of the phrase. At the second playing, the groups of triads forming these effects are symbolized as intimated by the slurs below the bass staff.

In dictating the exercises in three metre, extreme caution should be used in relating the triads preceding and succeeding the bar line. This is done by the *legato* grouping over the bar line, which should always be a factor in the playing of any phrase. The second pulse triad should be played as less intensely related to the preceding and succeeding triads and as standing between the first and third pulse triads; in fact, in the manner of an interpolated triad. The three metre phrase should always be dictated first for the semi- and full effects to be symbolized; and then the triads symbolized as making up these semi- and full effects. The exercises should then be dictated, omitting the second pulse triad, and permitting the first pulse to be sustained over the two pulses; each measure thereby containing the value of a half-note plus a quarter-note.

In all exercises taken from dictation, the student must use the symbols for the harmonic and melodic law. The writing of notes should be prohibited, except in the case of the soprano part.

In conjunction with the VI triad into which the III triad naturally progresses harmonically, the position of the III triad is auralized by its passing-tone character and its weak harmonic relationship to the key-centre.

These exercises, like the preceding ones, should be used as retentive memory exercises; when thus used the semi- and full effect symbolizing should precede the triad symbols.

These exercises include all of the diatonic consonant harmonic subject-matter of the major keys. The emotional effects of the constant use of concords (or triads) should be dwelt upon and aurally experienced, for it is felt, in all of these exercises, that the triads have no potent qualities, nor do they have any causal significance. They progress harmonically one into the other by virtue of their relationship in the harmonic law. There is nothing within their own structure which demands progression. They are therefore all resultant in quality, static in structural character, and their emotional use must be in accord with these characteristics and qualities. A good example of the static, resultant use of the triad is shown in the Palestrina Hymn, *The strife is o'er, the battle done.* The use of the triads in the hymn is absolutely in keeping with the meaning of the words.

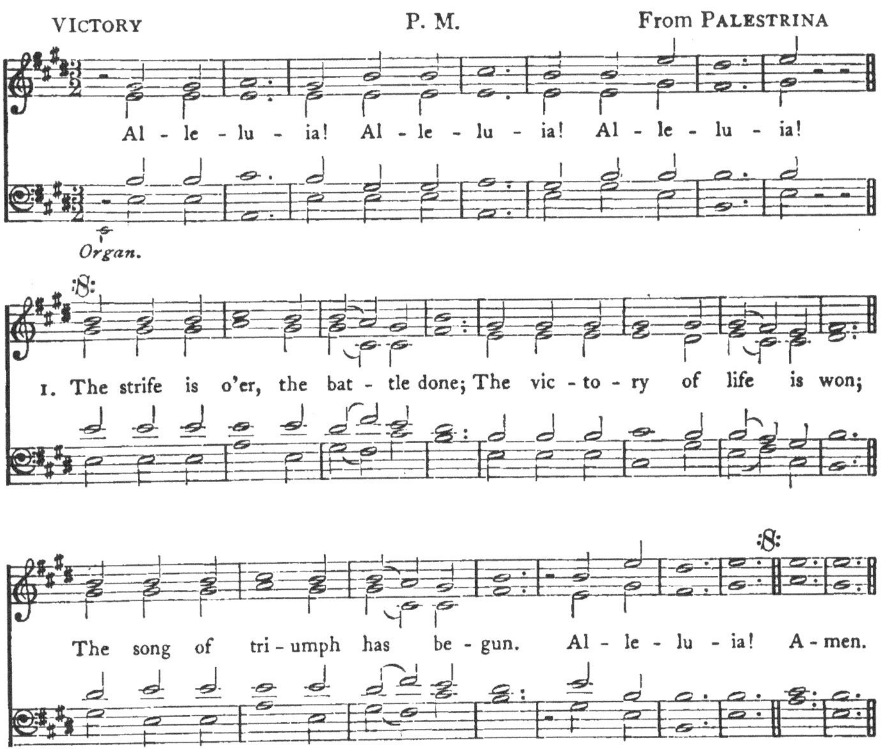


The various methods to be applied in working out the exercises are here enumerated in the order in which they are to be used.

(1) Auralization and symbolization of triads.

(2) Retentive memory work, symbolizing the effects (semi- and full), and writing symbols for harmonic and melodic laws before the notes are written.

(3) Keyboard work, in which the exercises are played from harmonic and melodic symbols, obscuring the written notes.

(4) Transposition of the exercises from one key to another. Each exercise should be played from the symbols of the harmonic and melodic laws in all keys.

(5) Original improvisation at the keyboard should be done in all keys. In this work the student should be required to use four-part structure *only*, and to keep soprano and alto parts in the right hand, tenor and bass parts in the left.

(6) Original improvisations, written after having been played. It is best to require the student to play an improvisation through twice before proceeding to write it.

The 3rd, 4th, 5th and 6th methods of using the subject-matter of this chapter should follow the complete mastery of the first two methods. These several methods of application should first be used in the phrase examples if the period examples are found to be too difficult.

8 5 4 2 3 4 2 3 4 4 2 3 2 1
I I II V I IV V I IV II V I V I
5 4 2 3 4 2 3 4 6 5 8 7 2 1
I II V I II V I IV IV I I V V I
1 2 3 4 4 2 3 5 6 5 5 4 2 1
I V I IV II V I I IV V I II V I
3 4 2 7 1 2 3 2 2 3 4 4 2 1
I IV V V I V I II V I IV II V I
8 5 4 2 3 4 2 3 4 2 3 2 7 1
I I II V I IV V I IV V I II V I
5 4 2 3 4 2 3 2 3 4 2 3 2 1
I II V I IV V I V I II V I V I

8 8 7 8 6 5 5 6 6 8 5 6 5 5
I IV V I II V I IV II I I IV V I
5 6 5 5 4 2 3 6 5 5 8 6 5 5
I IV V I II V I IV V I I II V I
8 2 3 5 4 2 3 2 2 3 4 2 7 8
I V I I II V I II V I IV V V I
3 5 4 3 2 3 4 2 3 2 4 2 5 5
I I II I V I IV V I II II V V I
8 5 6 6 1 2 3 2 2 1 5 4 2 1
I I IV II I V I II V I I II V I
3 4 2 3 2 2 3 4 4 2 3 2 7 8
I IV V I II V I IV II V I II V I

5 4 3 4 2 5 5 6 8 2 7 8 8 8
I II IV V V I IV IV II V I IV I
3 5 4 2 3 2 2 3 4 3 2 7 2 1
I I II V I II V I IV I II V V I
8 6 5 2 3 4 2 3 4 4 2 3 2 1
I II V V I IV V I IV II V I V I
5 3 2 2 3 4 2 3 4 4 2 3 2 1
I I II V I IV V I IV II V I V I
1 2 3 2 2 5 5 4 2 3 4 4 2 1
I V I II V V I II V I IV II V I
5 6 6 5 5 4 2 3 4 2 5 5 4 3
I IV II V I IV V I II V V I IV I

All of these exercises in two metre are of the period length, i.e., consisting of an antecedent and consequent phrase. They also start on the accented beat — in other words — on the thesis; before dictating the exercises in the different keys, the instructor should have the student erect the tones of the harmonic law of the key of the exercise, and require the I, V, IV and II triads to be spelled in each key. After these exercises have been written from dictation the notes, as written, should be covered by a strip of paper, the width of the staffs, allowing only the Roman numerals of the harmonic law, and the Arabic numerals of the melodic law to be visible; the student must be required to play the exercise in all keys to correspond to the symbols of both laws; in the work at the keyboard the soprano and alto voices ought to be played as far as possible by the right hand — the tenor and bass voices by the left hand. The attention of the student should be continuously turned toward the progression of the inner voices and the doubled tone of the triad; the outside voices (soprano and bass) are already intimated by the symbols; parallel faulty progression should be avoided in all cases. — In the retentive work, the student should be required to listen to the exercises as played by the instructor, and memorize the chord-succession, grouping the chords preceding and succeeding the bar lines, and tabulating these chord-successions by the use of the Roman numerals; after this has been accomplished, the melody of the given exercise should be tabulated by the use of the Arabic numerals ; no notes are to be written until the har monic and melodic laws have been thus memorized.

**EXERCISES IN THREE METRE EMPLOYING THE I, V, IV AND II TRIADS**

8 6 5 5 3 2 2 4 2 3 5 6 6 8 5 4 2 2 7 8
I II V I I II V IV V I I IV II I I IV V II V I
3 4 2 5 5 3 6 6 5 2 3 5 6 6 7 8 5 4 2 5 7 8
I II V V I I IV II V V I I IV II V I I II V V V I
8 7 8 2 3 2 2 7 8 2 3 2 7 8 6 2 7 5 7 8
I V I V I II V V I V I II V I IV II V V V I
5 6 6 5 5 8 2 3 4 4 2 3 2 1 7 8 6 2 2 4 2 1
I IV II V I I V I IV II V I II IV V I IV II V IV V I
8 5 3 4 2 5 5 6 8 8 6 2 7 8 5 3 4 2 5 5
I I I II V V I IV IV I II II V I I I IV V V I
6 5 4 2 3 4 6 5 3 4 2 3 2 2 5 5 6 2 7 5 7 8
IV I II V I IV IV I I II V I II V V I IV II V V V I

# *Aural Practice*

8 5 6 5 5 8 6 5 2 3 6 8 2 7 8 5 6 5 2 1
I I IV V I I II V V I IV IV II V I I IV V V I
3 2 3 4 4 2 5 5 6 5 5 8 8 2 7 8 5 3 4 2 7 1
I V I IV II V V I IV V I I IV II V I I I II V V I
5 4 2 3 2 7 1 2 3 2 2 3 4 3 5 6 5 2 7 1
I IV V I II V I V I V II I IV I I IV V V V I
2 3 4 2 3 5 6 5 4 2 3 5 6 6 5 5 3 4 2 7 2 1
V I II V I I IV I II V I I IV II V I I IV V V V I
5 6 6 5 2 3 4 2 5 5 5 6 6 8 5 6 5 2 7 8
I IV II V V I IV V V I I IV II I I IV V V V I
3 4 6 6 5 2 3 4 2 5 5 4 3 2 2 3 5 6 6 4 2 1
I IV IV II V V I IV V V I IV I II V I I IV II II V I

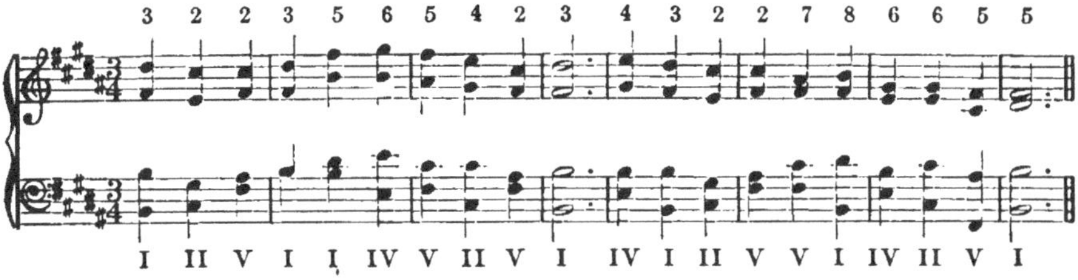
3 2 2 3 5 6 5 4 2 3 4 3 2 2 7 8 6 6 5 5
I II V I I IV V II V I IV I II V V I IV II V I

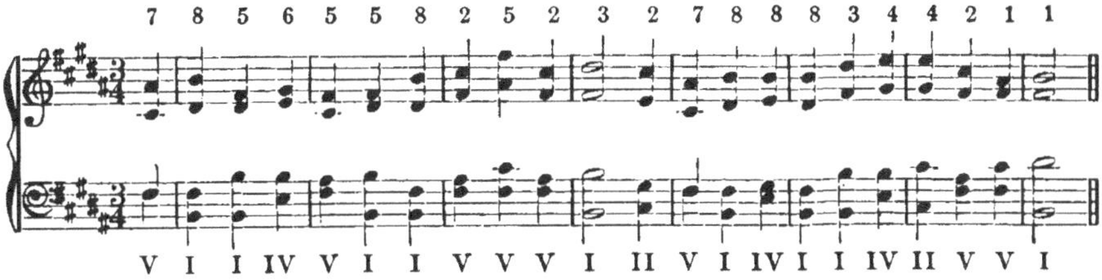
7 8 5 6 5 5 8 2 5 2 3 2 7 8 8 8 3 4 4 2 1 1
V I I IV V I I V V V I II V I IV I I IV II V V I

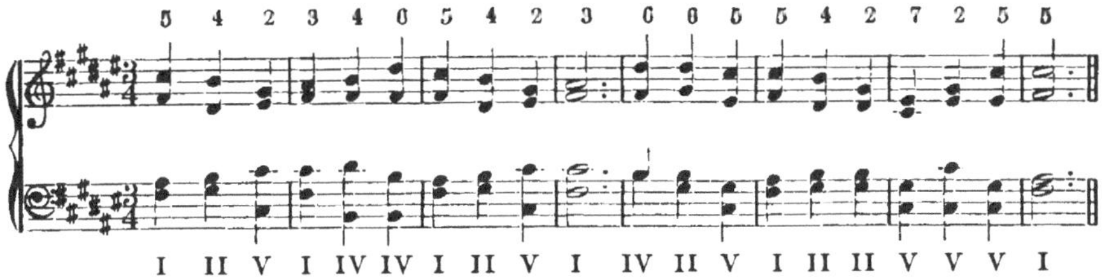
5 4 2 3 4 6 5 4 2 3 6 6 5 5 4 2 7 2 5 5
I II V I IV IV I II V I IV II V I II II V V V I

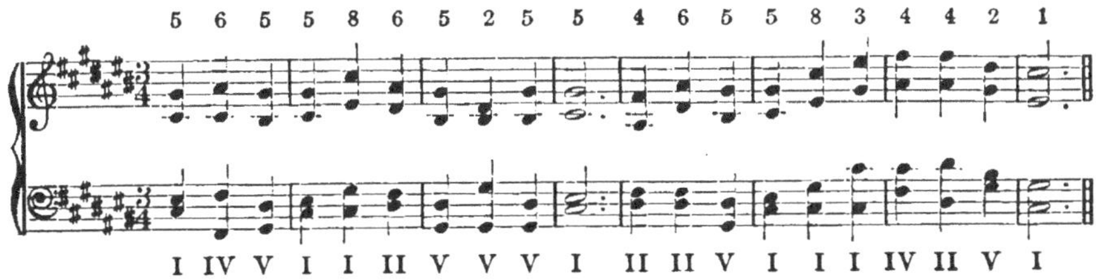
5 6 5 5 8 6 5 2 5 5 4 6 5 5 8 3 4 4 2 1
I IV V I I II V V V I II II V I I I IV II V I

## EXERCISES IN TWO AND THREE METRE EMPLOYING THE I, V, IV, II, VI AND III TRIADS

8 7 6 6 5 2 3 5 1 1 2 7 2 1
I III IV II V V I III VI IV II V V I

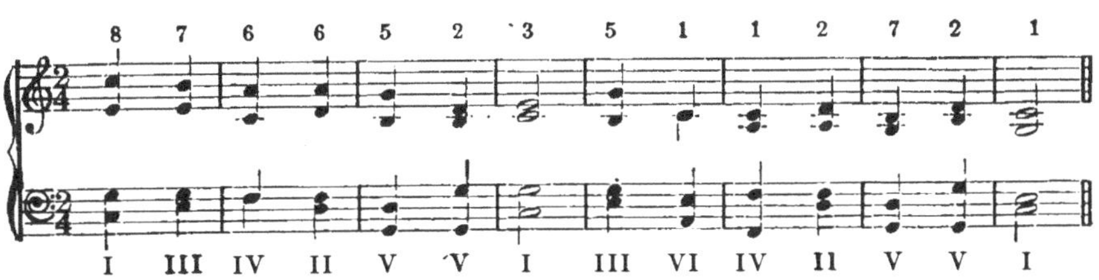

5 6 6 5 3 4 2 3 4 2 3 5 6 5 7 8 2 7 5 5
I VI IV V VI II V I II V I I IV V III VI II V V I
3 3 4 4 2 5 5 5 1 2 3 4 2 1
I VI IV II V V I III VI V I IV V I
5 4 2 3 3 4 2 3 4 2 5 1 2 3 3 4 4 2 7 1
I IV V I VI II V I IV V III VI V I VI IV II V V I
8 8 7 6 5 4 2 3 5 1 2 3 6 6 5 5 6 6 5 2 7 8
I VI III IV I II V I III VI V I IV II V I VI IV V V V I
1 2 7 8 4 2 5 5 6 6 5 5 4 2 7 1
VI V V I IV V V I IV II V I II V V I
5 4 2 5 5 3 5 1 4 3 2 2 7 2 3 4 4 2 7 2 5 5
I II V V I I III VI IV I V II V V I IV II II V V V I

5 1 2 3 4 2 3 5 5 4 6 5 7 8
I VI V I II V I III I II II V V I
3 3 4 2 3 5 1 4 2 3 4 2 4 3 2 1 1 2 7 8
I VI IV V I III VI IV V I II V IV I V VI IV II V I
8 7 6 5 8 2 5 5 4 2 7 8 8 2 7 8
I III IV I I V V I II V V I VI II V I
2 3 4 4 2 3 5 4 2 5 5 6 6 6 7 8 5 4 2 5 7 8
V I IV II V I III II V V I VI IV II V I I II V V V I
8 7 6 6 5 2 3 5 5 4 2 3 2 1
I III IV II V V I III I II V I V I
3 4 2 5 5 4 2 3 1 1 2 7 2 1
I IV V V I II V III VI IV II V V I

5 6 4 2 3 5 1 2 3 4 2 4 6 5 6 6 5 3 4 3
I VI II V I III VI V I IV V IV IV I VI IV V VI IV I
5 4 2 3 5 6 6 5 6 5 8 2 3 4 2 1
I II V I I IV II V IV I VI V I IV V I
6 5 8 2 3 4 4 2 3 4 2 8 8 2 7 8 7 6 6 5 2 3
IV I VI V I IV II V I IV V VI IV II V I III IV II V V I
5 6 6 5 5 8 2 1 5 6 6 5 7 8
I IV II V I VI V I I VI IV V V I
8 5 1 2 3 5 1 1 2 7 1 1 2 3 5 4 2 7 5 5
I I VI V I III VI IV II V I VI V I I II V V V I
8 2 5 5 6 6 5 5 3 2 1 1 2 7 2 1
VI V V I VI IV V I I II VI IV II V V I

In the dictation of the above exercises the student's ear should be constantly prompted to auralize the triads according to the distance they are separated from the key centre; the important position of the II triad must be constantly referred to, its position with regard to the key centre admitting only the V triad between it and the key centre. The VI triad should be fixed with regard to its position in the harmonic law by noting that the IV triad is standing next to it, and between it and the key centre. The III triad is felt to be so remote from the key centre, that it generally assumes the character of a passing chord.

# CHAPTER VIII

## THE PERIOD

The period in music is a melodic form, resulting from the addition of a second phrase to the first phrase. The second phrase is not merely an extension of the first phrase; it is rather an answer, or complement, to the first phrase. The first phrase of a period is called the antecedent. The added, or second phrase, is called the consequent.

The length of a phrase is determined by the presence of a cadence. Inasmuch as a period is defined as a large unit made up of two smaller units, it is imperative that the antecedent phrase should end with a half- or semi-cadence, while the cadence employed at the end of a consequent phrase should be a full cadence.

The aural effect desired at the semi-cadence is to mark the end of the antecedent phrase without aurally determining complete rest or ending. The cadence should be so formed as to imply that the consequent phrase is to follow. The full cadence at the end of the consequent phrase must aurally determine the effect of complete ending (close). This effect is best accomplished by the harmonic progression of the V triad into the I triad in octave-position. The full perfect and complete cadence is obviously most forcefully formed by the harmonic progression of the V chord into the I triad brought in the position of the eighth or octave.

Ex. 70.

Any triad may be the triad of resolution in a semi-cadence. The V triad, however, is best as the triad of resolution of a semi-cadence, because, being the most active triad of the key, it aurally determines the key-centre without producing upon the ear the effect of a complete close. The triad of resolution of the full cadence must always be the I triad, and this must always be used in the octave-position, as illustrated above.

The phrase, being generally four measures in length, is answered by a second phrase of the same length. Therefore, the period is generally of eight measures. The melodic figures of the second, or consequent phrase should conform to those used in the first or antecedent phrase, not merely in reiteration, but similar figures which may be discerned as determining unity in the melodic material should be so used as to produce a certain amount of variety. For example, the melodic figures of the consequent phrase may be those of the antecedent phrase inverted. The second, or consequent phrase, may, however, employ melodic figures which do not occur in the antecedent phrase. The cadences of both phrases must obviously be different. In the harmonic examples used in the preceding chapters, the period-form is employed in order to establish more forcefully the tonality of the exercises.

In employing the exercises for the writing of melodies, the chord-succession should be adhered to as represented by the harmonic symbols, but the soprano part is to be disregarded entirely. The melodic tones employed must be as far as possible harmonic tones of the chords determined by the symbols. It is imperative that the figures of which the melody is composed should begin with an harmonic tone and employ within its form, or contour, the tones of the harmony it is made to represent. Other tones called passing-tones may be employed in the formation of a figure, although not tones of the chord which the figure is made to represent. For example:

In each figure the chord is indicated by the Roman numeral. The tones marked with an asterisk are inharmonic tones.

All of them are introduced diatonically (stepwise) and are called passing-tones.

In writing melodies to the succession of chords of the previous exercises, the tones employed are to include harmonic tones and inharmonic passing-tones. Any figure resulting from the subdivision of the pulse may be employed, but great caution should be exercised not to use too many diversified figures in any melody.

In writing original melodies to form a period-length, the student should first determine the metre to be employed, and then exercise caution with regard to the rhythmic arrangement within each measure, remembering that the longer note-values should occur on the strong or resolution pulses, namely, the first pulse in each measure. Each figure employed should adequately outline the chord it is meant to represent, and each figure should begin with an harmonic tone.

All rules explained in the chapter on melody-writing as applied to the phrase are to be adhered to in writing melody for the period-length. The last factor of melody, namely, proportion, is now seen, for when the antecedent phrase and the consequent phrase are both of the same length, the proportion of melody is said to be regular. If, however, a four-measure antecedent phrase is answered by a three-measure consequent phrase, the proportion of the period is said to be irregular.

---

# CHAPTER IX

## INVERSION OF THE PRIMARY TRIAD

Inversion of a chord occurs when a tone other than its root appears in the bass part. All triads may appear in three positions:

First, the fundamental position, when the root of the triad appears in the bass;

Second, the first inversion, when the third of the triad appears in the bass;

Third, the second inversion, when the fifth of the triad appears in the bass.

In all of the exercises that have preceded this chapter, the triads have appeared in the fundamental position only. The symbol has been merely the Roman numeral. In the above illustration there are added, to the Roman symbols, small numerals at the lower right-hand corner, which indicate the inversions of the triad.

The reason for inverting a triad is, primarily, to permit its bass part to *act melodically* (that is, stepwise), thereby insuring a good melodic form. In scanning the previous exercises, the bass part is seen continuously to leap. This is due to the fact that the root of the triad in the fundamental position is a tone of the harmonic law; the tones of which law are separated from each other by intervals of thirds and fifths.

When the triad is inverted, the bass tone becomes either the third or the fifth of the triad, and these inverted bass tones will be found to act melodically (stepwise). Therefore, all of the tones of an inverted triad act melodically. The triad, however, will progress harmonically according to its root relationship, establishing the fact that the inversion of a triad does not affect the triad's harmonic relationship. For example, the inversions of the V triad will progress as follows:

The bass tone of the $V_1$ triad is the seventh of the scale, and its melodic progression to the eighth step takes place as the triad progresses harmonically to the I triad. Therefore, the bass of the $V_1$ triad progresses as the active seventh step of the melodic law, and not as the active seventh step of the harmonic law. Furthermore, the three upper voices progress diatonically, that is, according to the melodic law. It therefore follows that all of the tones of an inverted chord are melodic in character, and progress diatonically if possible. The example of the progression of the $V_2$ triad affirms the above conclusion. The second scale-step as the bass tone of the $V_2$ triad, possessing an active tendency either way, permits the $V_2$ triad to progress harmonically upward into the $I_1$ triad or downward into the I triad.

## THE FIRST INVERSIONS OF THE PRIMARY TRIADS

The tone which is best to double in the first inversion of any primary triad, is its root; next, its fifth; never its third, unless the outer parts *lead through* the doubled third of the inverted triad. Diatonic progression is then indulged in, and the scale is affirmed more strongly than would occur if the root or fifth of the inverted triad were doubled.

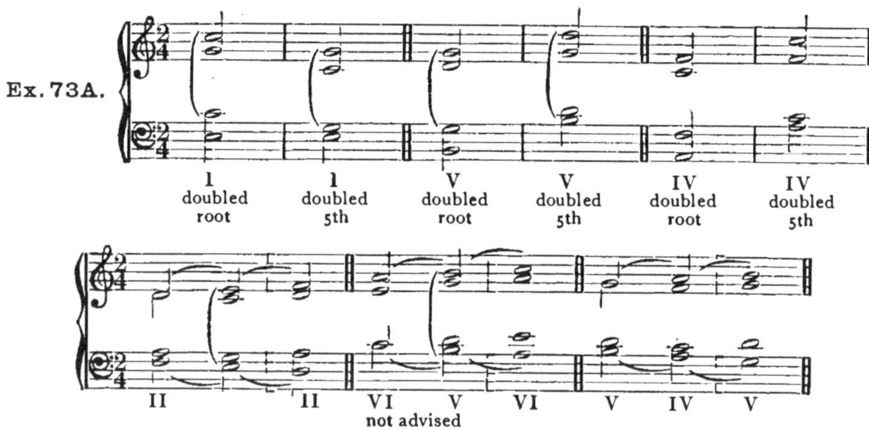


Diatonic progression of the outer parts, doubling the thirds in the first inversions of the primary triads I, V and IV.

In all of the above examples, the doubled tone in the inverted triad intimates the triad of the doubled tone (as in the case of the triad in the fundamental position); therefore, in the case of the doubled fifth in the first inversion of the I and the IV triads, these inverted triads may be made to intimate the coming of the V and the I triads; the doubling of the fifth in their inversions would therefore be better than the doubling of their roots. For example:

In both of these examples, the doubled fifths in the first inversion are better than the doubled roots would be, because in both instances the doubled tone intimates the triads which follow.

Smooth part-leading is always desirable, and should be sought for; but when it is possible so to use the doubled tone of any triad in the fundamental or first inverted position that the doubled tone foretokens the coming of the triad of that doubled tone, it is not only permissible, but advisable, to double the fifths of the triads rather than their roots.

In the first inversions of the primary triads the root is often found in soprano. The fifth of the triad may also be used in soprano, but the third of the triad never occurs in soprano unless introduced diatonically

The inversion of any triad adds another structural activity to those already cited. This is the last way in which any chord may be made structurally active. The other two ways are: (1) by placing any tone other than the root in the soprano; (2) by doubling any tone other than the root to procure the fourth part. All three ways of making a triad structurally active may be present at one time; or one or two may be present. Thus:

In the first $I_1$ triad, the structural activity is due only to the inversion of the triad. In the second $I_1$ triad, the structural

activity is due to two causes, namely, the inversion of the triad, and the doubled fifth of the triad. In the third $I_1$ triad, all of the structural activities are present, namely, the inversion of the triad, the doubled fifth of the triad, and the position of the fifth in soprano.

These structurally active qualities of the triad must be conscientiously auralized, and the difference in activity of all three carefully noted. The aural effect of doubling the fifth of the triad instead of the root, thereby unindividualizing the triad, is to be carefully auralized. This structural activity gives to the triad a naïveté in sound, due to the minimizing of its own individuality, by making it sound like the triad of the doubled tone. Such a structural fact is well adapted to the use of the triad in the writing of children's songs, where undeveloped qualities are depicted.

The first inversion of any triad makes it more pliable, as it structurally relates itself to other triads. The first inversion of all of the primary triads is extensively used and the triads used in this inverted form appear as triads of resolution, as well as harmonically progressing triads.

## THE SECOND INVERSION OF THE PRIMARY TRIADS

The second inversion of a triad occurs when its fifth is placed in the bass. This second inversion affects the triad by making it still more structurally active than was the case in the first inversion of the triad, because the triad in the second inversion seems to be aurally more independent of its root significance, having been turned twice upon itself. For this reason the use of the second inversion of the triad is more restricted than that of the first inversion. All primary triads may be employed in the second inversion. In the second inversion of a primary triad the fifth is almost always doubled to procure the fourth part. For example:

Ex. 76.

All these inversions, therefore, constantly possess at least two of the structural active qualities which an inverted triad may possess, besides the added activity due to the second inversion of the triad. Hence, their sound has a peculiarly active effect, for which reason their use in a phrase is limited. The active structural qualities that they all possess make it imperative to introduce them diatonically in the confines of the phrase. The diatonic use of the second inversions makes them appear as passing-tone harmonies, and not as real harmonies. They generally occur, therefore, in the confines of a phrase, between the first inversion and fundamental position of a reiterated triad. For example:

Ex. 77.

In all of the above examples, the second inversions of the I, IV and V triads appear between reiterated triads, and are harmonically progressing triads. They are seldom used as triads of resolution. The diatonic manner in which these triads in the second inversion are used lessens the structural activity they all possess. This lessening of their structural activity is imperative in the confines of a phrase. The only place in the phrase where this structural activity is useful is at the cadence, in other words, at the end of the phrase; for at this point the active qualities possessed by the second inversion of the triad are in keeping with the feeling of rushing to rest, which the structure of the phrase at this place most naturally possesses.

The authentic cadence is very often employed as the end of the phrase. This cadence is formed by the harmonic progression of the V triad into the I triad; therefore, the second inversion of the I triad, through its structural activity preceding the V triad, is a most adaptable form to use in this place in the phrase. The doubled fifth of the $I_2$ triad intimates the

V triad which succeeds the $I_2$ triad. In this place in the phrase, the $I_2$ triad may be introduced by a leap, which leap tends to accentuate the structural activity which the $I_2$ triad possesses.

Any second inversion of the primary triads may be introduced in the confines of the phrase by a leap, but only when such a second inversion is a repetition of the same primary triad. For example:

In Example *A*, the $I_2$ triad is introduced by a leap, because of the repetition of the I triad. In Example *B*, the $I_2$ triad is introduced by a leap, as part of the closing authentic cadence. Both of these uses of the $I_2$ triad are good.

## AURAL PRACTICE

In auralizing the examples at the end of this chapter, all of the methods given for aural practice in the preceding chapters are to be employed in their regular order. The structural activities possessed by the inverted triads are to be most carefully discerned.

## EXERCISES EMPLOYING THE INVERSIONS OF THE I, V AND IV TRIADS

1 1 2 3 5 3 4 3 2 3 2 1 2 3 1 1 3 2 7 8
I $I_1$ V I $V_1$ I $IV_1$ $I_2$ V I II VI V I $I_1$ $IV_1$ $I_2$ V V I
3 4 3 5 6 6 5 5 4 3 3 4 2 1
I $IV_2$ I $I_1$ IV II V I $IV_2$ I VI II V I
3 5 3 4 5 6 5 5 5 5 6 6 6 5 3 4 3 2 7 8
I $V_1$ I $IV_1$ $I_2$ IV $I_2$ V $V_1$ I VI IV II $V_1$ I $IV_1$ $I_2$ V V I
8 7 6 6 5 2 3 4 2 3 4 5 7 8
I III IV II $V_1$ V I II V I $IV_1$ $I_2$ V I
1 2 3 4 5 6 5 2 5 3 5 3 4 5 6 6 5 2 7 1
I V I $IV_1$ $I_2$ IV V V $V_1$ I $V_1$ I $IV_1$ $I_2$ IV II $V_1$ V V I
5 4 3 3 4 2 3 5 1 1 4 3 2 1
I $IV_2$ I VI IV V I III VI IV $IV_1$ $I_2$ V I

3 5 3 2 1 4 3 2 5 5 4 5 6 5 3 1 3 2 7 1
I V1 I V VI IV1 I2 V V1 I IV1 I2 IV I1 I IV1 I2 V V I
3 5 6 6 5 2 3 5 3 2 1 3 2 1
I I1 IV II V1 V I V1 I II VI I2 V I
5 4 3 6 5 5 3 4 6 5 5 8 6 5 3 4 3 1 7 8
I IV2 I IV I1 V1 I IV1 IV V I I1 IV I1 I IV1 I2 I2 V I
1 1 2 5 3 4 2 1 6 5 8 3 2 1
I I1 V V1 I II V I1 IV I VI I2 V I
3 4 3 6 5 2 3 4 5 6 6 5 2 1
I IV2 I IV I2 V I IV1 I2 IV II V1 V I
8 8 8 5 3 4 2 1 2 3 4 5 5 5
I IV2 I V1 I II V VI V I IV1 I2 V I

5 3 4 5 6 5 5 5 5 6 6 5 3 3 2 1
$V_1$ I $IV_1$ $I_2$ IV V $V_1$ I $I_1$ IV II $V_1$ I $I_2$ V I
3 4 6 5 5 8 6 6 5 2 3 5 6 5 2 3 5 1 3 2 7 8
I $IV_1$ IV V I $I_1$ IV II $V_1$ V I $I_1$ IV $V_1$ V I III VI $I_2$ V V I
8 8 3 4 5 3 2 1 2 3 4 3 2 1
I $IV_1$ $I_2$ IV $I_1$ I V $I_1$ $V_2$ I $IV_1$ $I_2$ V I
1 2 5 2 3 1 6 5 5 2 3 5 3 5 6 5 8 8 2 1 7 8
VI V $V_1$ $V_1$ I $I_1$ IV $I_2$ V V I $V_1$ I $I_1$ IV $I_1$ I VI II $I_2$ V I
3 5 3 4 2 3 6 5 5 6 6 8 8 3 2 1
I $V_1$ I II V I IV V $I_1$ IV II I $IV_1$ $I_2$ V I
3 2 1 1 2 7 8 1 2 3 4 4 5 3 5 1 3 2 7 8
I $V_2$ $I_1$ IV II V I VI V I II $IV_2$ $V_1$ I III $IV_1$ $I_2$ V V I

---

# CHAPTER X

## INVERSIONS OF THE SECONDARY TRIADS

It has been established in previous chapters that the triads, both primary and secondary, are of varying importance in any key. It has also been established that the secondary triad on the second degree is harmonically more important than the primary triad on the fourth degree, and that the other secondary triads, namely, the VI and the III, are less important harmonically than the primary triad on the fourth degree. The above facts are again cited for the purpose of determining how many inversions the secondary triads may undergo, for it must be apparent that the less related a chord becomes in a key, the less varied can the use of that chord be as regards inversion.

This principle obtains in determining the inversions of the secondary triads. Accordingly, the II triad should appear in both of its inversions, the VI triad possibly in only one inversion, namely, the first; while the III triad may never occur in any inversion as a chord mass.

### THE INVERSIONS OF THE II TRIAD

This triad has already been found to be most useful in the fundamental position, as is seen by its constant use in the preceding exercises. The first inversion of the II triad occurs very frequently, and is a most important triad-form. It occurs both as a triad of resolution, and as a harmonically progressing triad. The bass of the $II_1$ triad is always doubled when possible, and the tone which doubles the bass may be found in the soprano. The root of the $II_1$ triad is also found in the soprano. The fifth of the triad is less adaptable for use in soprano. The $II_1$ triad progresses harmonically upward into the V triad, or into the $I_2$ triad, or downward into the $I_1$ triad. For example:

The second inversion of the II triad is almost always, if not always, found as a passing-tone chord, and is seldom (if ever) found as a triad of resolution. When used as a passing-tone chord, it generally occurs between the $V_1$ and the V triad. No great importance, therefore, is attached to the $II_2$ triad.

In the above use of the $II_2$ triad, its passing-tone quality is seen by the diatonic progression of the bass and soprano. Often, in the place of the $II_2$ triad, the $IV_1$ triad with a doubled third is used, as in Example *B*.

### THE INVERSIONS OF THE VI TRIAD

The VI triad is seldom found in an inverted form. The $VI_1$ triad does occur, rarely, and when it is used, the bass of the triad (third of the chord) should be doubled, if possible. The $VI_1$ triad may be employed as the triad on the first beat of the consequent phrase. It progresses naturally into the $II_1$ triad, as illustrated at *A* in the example below·

Example *B* employs the $VI_1$ triad on the first pulse of the consequent phrase; the reiteration of the VI triad as in Example *B* is not advised, for such use of the secondary subject-matter, even in the case of the closely related II triad, is questionable, because of the minor qualities of the chords forming the relationship in a major key. It is liable to destroy the consciousness of the key's quality, and to imply a new key-centre, amounting thereby to a modulation. Thus it would seem that the VI triad is best confined in its use to the fundamental position.

The $VI_2$ triad is hardly possible, except as a passing-tone chord between the reiterated $II_1$ and II triads, which usage is of doubtful propriety, for the same reason as the analogous use of the VI triad.

Such triads as the $II_2$, $VI_2$ and $III_2$, should be auralized, but no harmonic significance attached to them. They are all merely passing-tone chords.

The III triad is never inverted; even in its fundamental position it takes upon itself the significance of a passing-tone chord. If such an aural significance is noted in a triad in fundamental position, it is unlikely that the triad may ever undergo inversion. The III triad in the fundamental position, however, is often employed as the first chord of the consequent phrase, and when used in this position, let the third of the triad be doubled, if possible. When the triad is employed, as it often is, between the I triad and the IV triad, it assumes the significance of a passing-tone chord. For example:

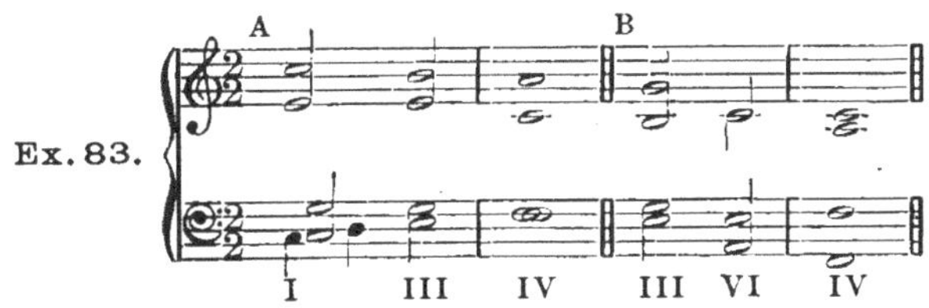


In Example *A* of the above illustration, the progression of the soprano is diatonic; that of the bass is also intimated as diatonic, which is easily discovered by subdividing the first pulse and using, instead of the bass tone C, the quarter-notes C and D, as written. In Example *B* it is noted that the III triad is made to progress according to the steps of the harmonic law, namely, to the VI triad. If the III triad, even placed upon the first pulse of the consequent phrase, were to progress to the $V_2$ triad, the III triad would assume the significance of a passing-tone chord.

To sum up the uses of the inversions of the secondary triads, it is found that the less closely related a triad is to its key-centre, the less varied it can appear. The II triad appears in the fundamental position and first inversion; the VI triad only in fundamental position (very rarely in the first inversion); the III triad rarely appears even in the fundamental position as an harmonic chord mass. The second inversions of all secondary triads are merely passing-tone chords, and are not considered as harmonic chord masses.

The proof that any chord forms a legitimate tone-group is, that it can appear as a chord of resolution as well as a chord progressing harmonically. It must be capable of assuming both relationships.

## AURAL PRACTICE

The aural practice of this chapter is identical with that laid down for the aural practice of the chapter on the inversion of the primary triads. The character of the triad should be auralized (whether major or minor); then its harmonic relationship to the key-centre, to determine whether it is a V, IV, or II triad; then the form in which it is presented is noted (whether the triad is in the fundamental position or inverted). This fact is determined by the kind of structural activity the triad possesses. In order to train the ear in the discernment of structural activity, due to the inversion of the triad, all the inverted triads should be placed, first, in their fundamental position, then in the first inversion, and also in their second inversion, and the ear taught to discern the structural activities resulting from the different positions. All other methods of practice, namely, memory, keyboard work, transposition, improvising, should be continued.

The writing of melodies to the exercises in this chapter should be conscientiously done. The soprano part, as it appears in all of the exercises, is to be discarded, and merely the chord-relationship retained. In providing melodies to these exercises, inharmonic passing-tones may be used. In addition to the inharmonic tones, the melodies of this chapter must be so written as to include the melodic structural effect called a sequence. A melodic sequence is the repetition of a series of tones, a tone higher or a tone lower than the original group. For example:

Sequences are to be written to the given harmonies of this chapter. In writing original melodies in this chapter, the III triad is used only to harmonize the seventh step, as it progresses diatonically downward to the sixth step.

**EXAMPLES, EMPLOYING THE INVERSIONS OF ALL TRIADS**

3 3 2 2 1 2 7 7 1 6 2 1 7 8
I VI₁ II V₁ I II₁ V III VI₁ II II I₂ V I
5 4 3 2 3 4 2 5 3 2 5 1 2 3 2 4 3 2 7 8
I IV₂ I II₁ VI₂ II V V₁ I V III VI V I II₁ II I₂ V V I
8 5 3 2 3 4 2 2 3 4 4 3 2 1
I I₁ I₂ V I II₁ V II₁ VI₂ II II₁ I₂ V I
8 8 8 3 2 1 1 2 7 1 6 7 8 2 2 1 1 2 7 8
I I₁ IV₁ I₂ V VI IV II V I VI₁ III₂ VI II V₁ I I₂ II₁ V I
4 3 2 3 2 1 2 3 5 4 2 3 2 1 7 1
IV₁ II₂ V I II₁ I₂ V I I II V I II₁ I₂ V I
3 2 7 1 2 3 4 4 3 2 1 2 4 2 3 2 1 3 2 1
I II₁ V I₁ V₂ I IV IV₁ I V VI II₁ II V I II₁ I₂ I₂ V I

5 8 6 4 3 2 3 2 3 4 4 2 7 8
I $I_1$ IV $II_1$ $I_2$ V I $II_1$ $VI_2$ II $II_1$ V V I
3 4 5 6 5 3 1 2 1 2 3 3 4 5 2 3 5 1 3 1 7 8
I $IV_1$ $I_2$ IV $I_1$ I VI $II_1$ $I_2$ V I $VI_1$ II $V_1$ V I III VI $I_2$ $I_2$ V I
3 4 3 2 1 2 3 2 3 4 2 1 7 8
I $IV_2$ I $II_1$ $I_2$ V I $II_1$ $VI_2$ II $II_1$ $I_2$ V I
2 3 4 6 5 5 1 3 2 5 3 2 7 1 4 3 2 1 6 4 2 3
V I $IV_1$ IV V I $IV_1$ $I_2$ V $V_1$ I $II_1$ V $I_1$ $IV_1$ $I_2$ V $I_1$ IV $II_1$ V I
3 2 7 1 6 5 5 1 2 3 2 1 7 1
I $II_1$ V $I_1$ IV V I VI V I $II_1$ $I_2$ V I
3 2 1 6 5 1 3 2 5 3 4 5 6 5 3 1 2 1 7 1
I $V_2$ $I_1$ IV $I_1$ $IV_1$ $I_2$ V $V_1$ I $IV_1$ $I_2$ IV $I_1$ I VI $II_1$ $I_2$ V I

8 7 6 4 3 2 3 2 3 4 4 3 2 1
$I$ $III$ $IV$ $II_1$ $I_2$ $V$ $I$ $II_1$ $VI_2$ $II$ $II_1$ $I_2$ $V$ $I$
5 8 2 3 3 2 1 7 2 3 6 7 8 2 7 8 6 4 2 3
$I$ $I_1$ $V$ $I$ $VI$ $II_1$ $I_2$ $V$ $V$ $I$ $VI_1$ $III_2$ $VI$ $II_1$ $V$ $I_1$ $IV$ $II_1$ $V$ $I$
3 5 6 4 3 2 3 2 3 4 5 3 3 1
$I$ $I_1$ $IV$ $II_1$ $I_2$ $V$ $I$ $II_1$ $VI_2$ $II$ $V_1$ $I$ $V$ $I$
2 7 1 2 3 3 4 3 2 5 3 6 5 3 4 5 6 4 3 2 7 8
$II_1$ $V$ $I_1$ $V$ $I$ $VI$ $II_1$ $I_2$ $V$ $V_1$ $I$ $IV$ $I_1$ $I$ $IV_1$ $I_2$ $IV$ $II_1$ $I_2$ $V$ $V$ $I$
5 6 4 2 3 4 2 7 5 5 8 6 4 3 2 3
$I$ $IV$ $II_1$ $V$ $I$ $II$ $II_1$ $V$ $V$ $I$ $I_1$ $IV$ $II_1$ $I_2$ $V$ $I$
5 3 4 2 7 8 8 8 2 2 3 3 4 5 2 3 7 8 2 1 7 8
$V_1$ $I$ $IV_1$ $II_1$ $V$ $I_1$ $VI$ $IV$ $II$ $V$ $I$ $VI_1$ $II$ $V_1$ $V$ $I$ $III$ $VI$ $II_1$ $I_2$ $V$ $I$

8 5 6 4 3 2 3 2 3 4 5 3 2 1
I $I_1$ IV $II_1$ $I_2$ V I $II_1$ $VI_2$ II $V_1$ I V I
5 4 3 2 7 1 1 3 2 3 5 5 2 3 4 6 5 7 2 1
I $IV_2$ I $II_1$ V $I_1$ $I_2$ $I_2$ V I III $V_1$ V I $IV_1$ IV $I_2$ V V I
3 4 5 6 4 3 2 3 5 1 2 3 4 5 7 8
I $IV_1$ $I_2$ IV $II_1$ $I_2$ V I III VI V I $IV_1$ $I_2$ V I
5 1 2 3 4 2 1 2 5 3 2 2 5 3 1 1 3 2 7 8
I $I_1$ V I $VI_1$ $II_1$ $I_2$ V $V_1$ I $II_1$ V $V_1$ I $I_1$ $IV_1$ $I_2$ V V I
8 5 3 4 2 5 3 4 5 6 4 3 2 1
I $I_1$ $I_2$ $II_1$ $V_2$ $V_1$ I $IV_1$ $I_2$ IV $II_1$ $I_2$ V I
8 8 6 5 5 4 3 2 5 3 4 5 6 5 5 4 3 2 7 8
I VI IV $I_1$ I $II_1$ $I_2$ V $V_1$ I $IV_1$ $I_2$ IV V I $II_1$ $I_2$ V V I

---

# CHAPTER XI

## DISCORDS

In beginning the study of the discords, the attention of the student is again called to the Chord of Nature, which was discussed in the chapter on intervals.

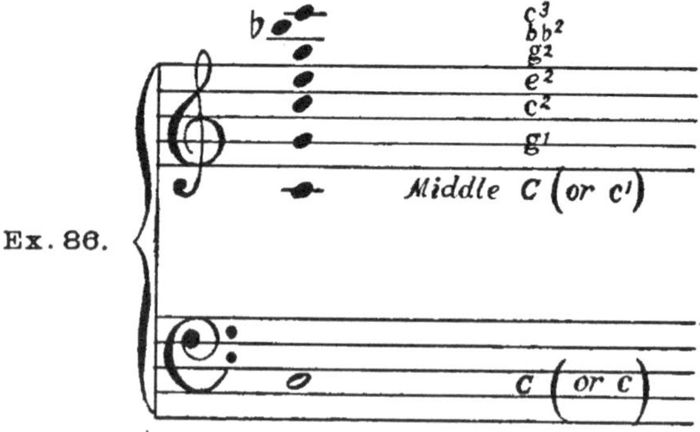


It is observed that the overtones of the fundamental C (c) falling between the duplicating overtones $c^2$ and $c^3$ are the overtones $e^2$, $g^2$ and $b^2$♭. These overtones, with $c^2$ as their root-tone, determine the types of chords that are possible in music.

The first type, namely, the triad, has already been defined and discussed. This type of chord is composed of the root-tone $c^2$ and the overtones $e^2$ and $g^2$, a third and fifth above the root-tone. The triad was found to be a concord.

The second type of chord possible in music is composed of the root-tone $c^2$ and the overtones $e^2$, $g^2$, and $b^2\flat$. This new type of chord is composed of the intervals of a third, fifth and minor seventh above the root-tone $c^2$. It therefore possesses in its structure a dissonant interval which distinguishes this type of chord from the triad (which is a concord). The seventh-chord is, therefore, found to be a discord.

The four-tone chord represented by the second type of chord is called a seventh-chord, by virtue of possessing within its structure the dissonance of a minor seventh. The interval which enters any chord-structure to make that chord a dissonant chord is, therefore, always a minor seventh. No other dissonant interval can ever be part of the structure of a diatonic dissonant chord, for in the Chord of Nature (seen above) the overtones which fall between $c^2$ and $c^3$ are the only ones which group themselves in thirds, and the last overtone so to relate itself within this octave is the overtone $b^2\flat$; after the appearance of the overtone B flat another repetition C of the fundamental appears, namely $c^3$. This closes the series of overtones which are related to one another in intervals of thirds. This was found to be the case in the classification of intervals as perfect consonances, imperfect consonances, and dissonances, In like manner the duplicating overtone $c^3$ closes the class of possible chord-structures, namely, triads or three-tone chords (concords) and seventh-chords, or four-tone chords (discords), in which the dissonant interval is always a minor seventh.

Hence, all triads (concords) may have added to them another tone, a third above their fifth, which added tone must form a minor seventh with the root-tone. Employ the triads, and add to each the tone forming a seventh with its root.

The symbol for all of these resulting chords is seen to be that used for the triad with the figure 7 added at the upper right-hand corner. In group *A* are placed the primary triads of the key of C, to which are added tones making these triads over into seventh-chords. In the $I^7$ chord the added tone B forms, with the root C of the chord, an interval of a major seventh. Therefore, a seventh-chord on the first degree of any scale is impossible, because the dissonance entering the structure of the $I^7$ chord is a major seventh, and not a minor seventh. In the $V^7$ chord the dissonance of a seventh which enters the chord-structure is found to be a minor seventh. Therefore this $V^7$, or dominant seventh-chord, is possible in every key. In the $IV^7$ chord the dissonance which enters its structure is found to be a major seventh, therefore a seventh-chord on the fourth degree is impossible.

It is noted that these seventh-chords result from adding a tone to the primary triads of the key, which tone is a seventh above their roots; it follows that a primary seventh-chord is one which results from adding a seventh to a primary triad; and according to the above results the only primary seventh-chord which is possible is the $V^7$ chord, called the dominant seventh-chord.

There is also an aural proof of the non-existence of a $I^7$ and a $IV^7$ chord, by experiencing the activity of the tone forming a major seventh with the roots of the $I^7$ and $IV^7$ chords, due to a lack of relationship of the tone forming the major seventh with the other chord-elements. If the $I^7$ chord in C major is played, the tone B will evince a tendency for resolution upward into the tone C while the other tones comprising the chord remain at rest. In the case of the $IV^7$ chord in the key of C, the tone E will seek resolution downward into the tone D, while the other chord-tones remain at rest. In contrast to the above two experiences, play the $V^7$ chord in the key of C, and no such preliminary resolution of any tone of the chord will be demanded, but the chord will seek resolution as a unit, proving that all its tones are true tones of a chord-structure, related naturally to the root-tone G.

It follows that, if within a chord-mass any tone seeks progression before the chord as a whole resolves, that tone, because of such active tendency, does not belong to the chord, or, in other words, is not an harmonic tone of the chord, but is a tone foreign to the chord-structure, known as an inharmonic tone. Such a tone in its relation to the chord-structure, seeks, through its activity, to progress to a legitimate tone of the chord-structure, before the chord as a unit resolves. To chord-structures possessing inharmonic tones, the so-called $I^7$ and $IV^7$ chords belong. These chords will eventually be seen to be a I triad with a passing seventh step of the scale, — and a $II^7$ chord in the first inversion with a passing third step of the scale.

The group of seventh-chords marked B in the example at the beginning of this chapter are formed by adding, to the secondary triads of the key, a fourth tone, which forms a seventh with the roots. In all of these chords the added tone forms a minor seventh with the root; therefore, the secondary $II^7$, $VI^7$, $III^7$ and $VII^7$ chords are possible in all keys and will be discussed in due time.

It would naturally follow (inasmuch as there is but one primary seventh-chord, while four secondary seventh-chords are possible), that there should be a distinctive aural difference between the primary seventh-chord and the secondary seventh-chords. This aural difference undoubtedly arises from the fact that a primary triad is the chord-base, so to speak, from which the primary dissonance is formed; whereas, in the case of the secondary dissonances, the secondary triads form the chord-base from which they were derived. It was noted that in the use of the secondary triads in major, the thirds of the triads are doubled. This doubled tone undoubtedly serves to soften or coerce their strident, harsh and unyielding character by tending to uncharacterize them. But when these triads are used as a chord-base upon which to build seventh-chords, the resulting chord will in consequence be a four-part structure, and no doubling will occur to soften or coerce their sound.

Therefore, the auralization of the secondary seventh-chords will result in experiencing a set of harsh, unyielding chords, in contrast to the pliable, soft, coercive sound of the primary seventh-chord.

Another significant structural difference between the primary and secondary seventh-chords is found in the intuitive capacity of the normal musical person to sing the root of the primary seventh-chord, whether in the fundamental or inverted position; whereas, in the case of the secondary seventh-chords, the root is often undiscernible, and therefore unsingable, even when thoughtfully sought, or a desire to sing the root is determined upon.

As previously pointed out, all consonances "progress," while all dissonances "resolve." Therefore, a seventh-chord is always spoken of as "resolving." It has also been pointed out in the chapter on intervals that all consonances are static, all dissonances dynamic; therefore, a seventh-chord is a dynamic chord, and aurally desires resolution, whereas a triad is static and aurally desires no progression. These characteristics are structural, and result from the possession, or non-possession, by the chord, of a dissonance.

The dynamic quality of dissonant chords (seventh-chords), and the static quality of consonant chords (triads), are facts of prime importance in musical composition. The seventh-chords, being dynamic, are causal; the triads, being static, are resultant. The potency of the seventh-chords cannot be interchanged for the impotency of the triads.

It is therefore seen that the emotional significance of a chord primarily depends upon its structural character (whether a discord or a concord), and its legitimate use is undoubtedly dependent upon this fact.

# CHAPTER XII

## THE DOMINANT SEVENTH-CHORD

This primary seventh-chord is the seventh-chord upon the fifth of the scale (symbol, $V^7$). Its harmonic resolution within the key is always into the I triad, for it is built upon the most active tone of the harmonic law, namely, the fifth degree. The chord elements are two in number, (1) the harmonic fifth degree and (2) the melodic seventh, second and fourth degrees. Inasmuch as its only resolution is into the I triad, the tones of the $V^7$ chord will progress, as the chord resolves, as follows: The harmonic fifth degree will leap down a fifth or up a fourth; the melodic seventh degree will progress upward to the eighth degree; the melodic second degree will progress up or down into the third or first degree; and the melodic fourth step will progress down into the third degree. To il lustrate:

Ex. 88.

In the above example it is apparent that the melodic second step as part of the $V^7$ chord cannot progress upward, for then the third of the primary I triad would be doubled. Again, if this melodic second step is allowed to progress downward, its action will result in tripling the root-tone of the I triad. The triad with a tripled root is at best merely an implied chord-structure, for there are obviously only two tones of the scale present (the tripled root-tone, and the third of the triad). This is not, therefore, a good chord-structure for a triad. In order to obviate such a presentation of the triad of resolution, the $V^7$ chord may appear without the second degree, and instead of this omitted degree, the root-tone doubled. To illustrate:

In this example, the harmonic root-tone G, in the bass of the $V^7$ chord, progresses by leaping a fourth upward to the root-tone C of the I triad. The melodic tone G, in the tenor, which duplicates the root-tone of the $V^7$ chord, is a melodic rest tone, and stays at rest in the resolution of the $V^7$ chord. The melodic seventh degree, in the alto of the $V^7$ chord, progresses upward to the eighth degree. The melodic fourth degree, in the soprano of the $V^7$ chord, progresses downward to the third degree. It is thus seen that the triad resulting from the resolution of the $V^7$ chord, from whose structure the second degree of the scale has been omitted, is a complete triad. This shows that the best way in which to present the $V^7$ chord in fundamental position is without its fifth, which is the second degree of the scale. This is done in order that the triad of resolution, namely, the I triad, shall appear complete. It will be found possible to omit the fifth (second degree of the scale) of the $V^7$ chord in all cases, except when the fifth of the chord (second degree of the scale) appears in soprano. It is then a given part, and cannot be omitted. In such case the seventh degree of the scale (the third of the $V^7$ chord) may be denied its natural progression upward to the eighth degree, and may progress downward into the fifth degree of the scale, a major third below. This unnatural progression of the seventh degree finds aural compensation in the fact that the natural progression of the seventh degree is transferred to another part in the triad of resolution. This part is obviously the eighth degree of the scale, which becomes the tone of resolution of the progressing second degree in the soprano of the $V^7$ chord. It is also the implied tone of resolution of the seventh degree, as one of the inner parts of the $V^7$ chord. To illustrate:

Ex. 90.

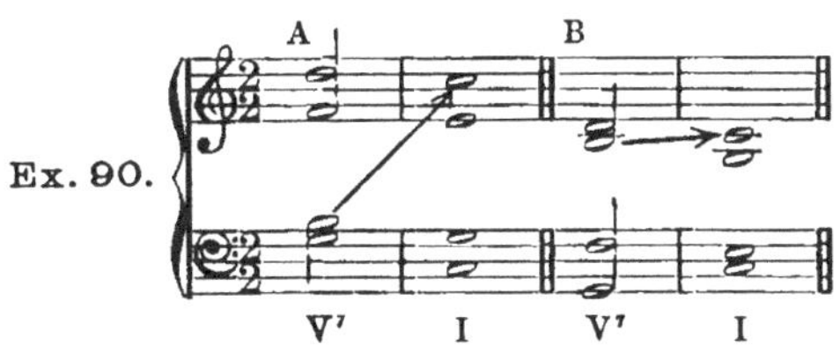


In the above illustration example *B* may be considered as the better, inasmuch as the soprano tone used as the transferred tone of resolution of the seventh degree occurs in the same register as the legitimate tone of resolution of the seventh degree would be found. In Example *A*, however, the transferred tone is an octave higher than the legitimate tone of resolution. In the exercises at the end of this chapter the transferred resolution of the seventh degree has been generally indulged in.

## AURAL PRACTICE

In auralizing the $V^7$ chord, its dissonant quality as contrasted with the consonant quality of all triads should be determined first. The qualities of chords are to be aurally determined as consonant major or minor triads, and dissonant $V^7$ chords. The fundamental position in which the dominant seventh-chord is always given in these exercises should be auralized by the demand that the chord makes upon the ear for a leaping progression of the root-tone in its bass. This aural feeling should be determined by the positive affirmation of the key-centre resulting from the harmonic resolution of the bass, which firm, secure feeling will never result from the resolution of an inverted $V^7$ chord. The fundamental position of the $V^7$ chord is the best for securing a full, perfect and complete cadence; then the bass part will affirm, in its progression, the *harmonic* law, whereas in an inverted $V^7$ chord all the tones are found to be *melodic* in character (as in the case of the triad), and the harmonic law will not be aurally represented by any tone, but merely implied through the harmonic action of the chord as it resolves to the I triad.

The complete close which results from the resolution of the dominant seventh-chord in fundamental position into the

I triad in the position of the eighth, is to be used only for the closing cadence of the consequent phrase. This relationship of chords is not good within the confines of the phrase.

The methods of presenting the subject-matter of this chapter are those employed in the preceding chapters. Melody-writing should be more varied in figure, and sequential melodic figures should be employed freely. The harmonies, having become more numerous and varied, will admit of more extensive use of rhythmic figures. The only inharmonic tone to be used at present is the passing-tone.

**EXERCISES EMPLOYING INVERTED TRIADS AND DOMINANT SEVENTH-CHORD**

4 3 2 1 6 5 4 3 2 4 3 6 5 3 4 2 3 2 1 3 2 1
V7 I V2 I1 IV I1 II1 I2 V V7 I IV I1 I II V I II1 I2 I2 V7 I
1 2 3 2 1 2 3 3 4 5 1 3 2 1
I V I II1 I2 V I VI IV I1 IV1 I1 V7 I
5 6 5 5 4 3 6 5 4 3 5 5 4 3 2 1 2 1 7 8
I IV V7 I IV2 I IV I2 V7 I III V1 V7 I II VI II1 I2 V7 I
5 6 5 5 4 3 2 3 6 5 4 2 3 4 2 1
I IV V7 I II1 I2 V I IV I1 II1 V I IV V7 I
5 4 3 5 1 4 3 2 3 4 4 3 2 1
I IV2 I III VI V7 I II1 VI2 II V7 I V7 I
8 6 5 4 3 5 4 3 2 4 3 8 2 7 5 5 6 2 1 3 2 1
I1 IV V7 V7 I I1 II1 I2 V V7 I VI II1 V V7 I IV II I2 I2 V7 I

6 5 4 3 2 1 2 3 3 4 4 3 5 1 2 1
IV $I_1$ $V^7$ I $II_1$ $I_2$ V I VI IV $V^7$ I III VI $V^7$ I
3 2 1 4 4 3 2 2 5 3 4 5 6 5 4 3 3 4 7 8
I $V_2$ $I_1$ IV $V^7$ I II V $V_1$ I $IV_1$ $I_2$ IV $V^7$ $V^7$ I $I_2$ $V^7$ $V^7$ I
8 7 6 6 5 4 3 2 2 3 5 4 2 1
I III IV II $V^7$ $V^7$ I $II_1$ V I $I_1$ $II_1$ $V^7$ I
3 4 6 5 4 3 2 1 2 3 5 6 6 8 5 1 3 4 2 1
I $IV_1$ IV $V^7$ $V^7$ I $II_1$ $I_2$ V I $I_1$ IV II I I $IV_1$ $I_2$ $V^7$ $V^7$ I
8 5 3 4 3 6 5' 5 4 3 3 4 2 1
I $I_1$ $I_2$ $V^7$ I IV V I $IV_2$ I VI $II_1$ $V^7$ I

# CHAPTER XIII

## INVERSIONS OF THE DOMINANT SEVENTH-CHORD

The dominant seventh-chord, being a four-tone chord, can undergo three inversions. The first inversion occurs when the third of the chord, which is the seventh degree of the scale, is in the bass. The second inversion occurs when the fifth of the chord, or second degree of the scale, is in the bass. The third inversion occurs when the seventh of the chord, which is the fourth degree of the scale, is in the bass. It has been previously shown that a chord is inverted to make the bass progress melodically; therefore, the bass tones of the inversions of the dominant seventh-chord will progress melodically to the rest tones of the I triad, according to their melodic active tendencies.

### THE FIRST INVERSION

In the first inversion of the V$^7$ chord the seventh degree of the melodic scale is in the bass. Therefore, its first inversion will resolve into the I triad as follows:

All the parts of the VI$^7_1$ chord are seen to act melodically; the bass progresses upward, being the active seventh degree of the melodic scale; the tenor remains stationary, being a rest tone; the alto progresses downward, being the active second degree of the melodic scale; the soprano progresses downward, being the active fourth degree of the melodic scale. This first inversion of the V$^7$ chord, therefore, resolves upward to the I triad in the fundamental position.

In auralizing this inversion, the strong active melodic tendency of the bass is to be determined, and attention is to be called to the upward progression of the bass into the I triad in fundamental position.

## THE SECOND INVERSION OF THE $V^7$ CHORD

In this second inversion the second degree of the melodic scale is in the bass. Therefore, the resolutions of the $V^7_2$ chord into the I triad are as follows:

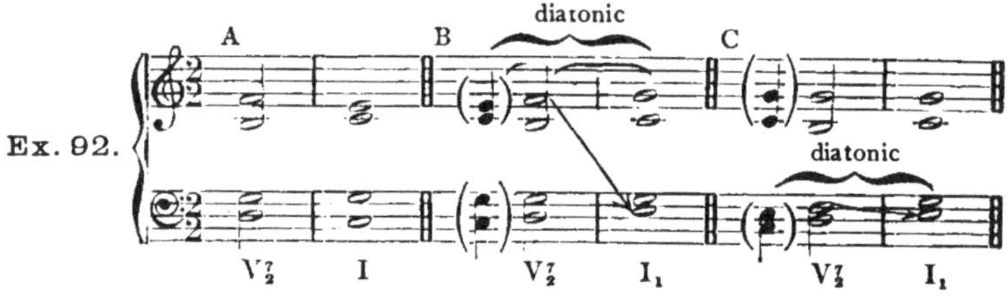

Ex. 92.

It is seen, in all these examples, that the parts of the $V^7_2$ chord act melodically. In Example *A*, the melodic parts progress in the direction of their natural resolution. In Example *B*, the soprano tone F, fourth degree of the scale, progresses upward against its natural resolution. The $V^7_2$ chord in this position, when progressing to the $I_1$ triad, must be preceded by the I triad in the position of the third; then the fourth degree will progress diatonically, and its upward progression, instead of its downward progression, is permitted. In this progression of the $V^7_2$ chord there is also the transferred resolution of this fourth degree, its tone of resolution being taken by the tone in the bass. In Example *C*, the parts of the $V^7_2$ chord follow their natural progression, with the exception of the tone *F* in the tenor. This fourth degree progresses upward instead of downward, but its tone of resolution is again transferred to the bass, in the same register. This example is better than the preceding one, although both are correct.

In auralizing the $V^7_2$ chord, the fact to be noted is the indifferent feeling with regard to the direction of the resolution of the $V^7_2$ chord; because of this indifference in directional resolution a certain complacency and lessening of dissonant quality will be noted, which is characteristic of the $V_2^7$ chord. It is obviously imperative to be mindful of the position of the I triad (resolution triad), whether it occurs in the fundamental position, or in the first inversion. The specific quality resulting from the indifferent resolution of the $V_2^7$ chord, which is its emotional significance, is that of complacency, apathy, indifference, and the like, in contrast to the intense, virile, decisive, emotional significance of the $V_1^7$ chord.

## THE THIRD INVERSION OF THE $V^7$ CHORD

In the third inversion of the $V^7$ chord the fourth degree of the melodic scale is in the bass. Therefore, the resolution of the $V_3^7$ chord into the $I_1$ triad will be as follows:

It is seen in the above example that all the parts of the $V_3^7$ chord act melodically:

The bass, fourth degree of melodic scale, proceeds down ward,

The tenor, second degree of melodic scale, proceeds downward,

The alto, fifth degree of melodic scale, remains at rest,

The soprano, seventh degree of melodic scale, moves upward.

It is also found that this inversion of the $V^7$ chord always resolves downward into the $I_1$ triad, owing to the presence of the active fourth degree of the melodic scale in the bass.

In auralizing the $V_3^7$ chord, the fact to be noted is its determined resolution downward into the first inversion of the I triad. There results from this determined resolution, an emotional quality of virility and intensity, which heightens the dissonant quality of this inversion (as in the case of the $V_1^7$ chord, in its determined upward resolution).

Any melodic tone of any of the inversions may be placed in the soprano, excepting the tone which would duplicate the bass tone of the chord. It is seen in all of the examples of the inverted $V^7$ chord that the chord is presented with all of its parts present. This is not because of its resolution, but because of an uncertainty or indefiniteness as to the identity of the chord, which would arise if any part of the inverted $V^7$ chord were to be omitted. This structural uncertainty is not an artistic asset in the use of any chord, and should be avoided.

In the use of the inversions of the dominant seventh-chord, care should be exercised in the repetition of the inverted chord not to produce an aural anticlimax by permitting the complacent $V^7_2$ inversion to become the chord of resolution of either the $V^7_1$ or the $V^7_3$ chords.

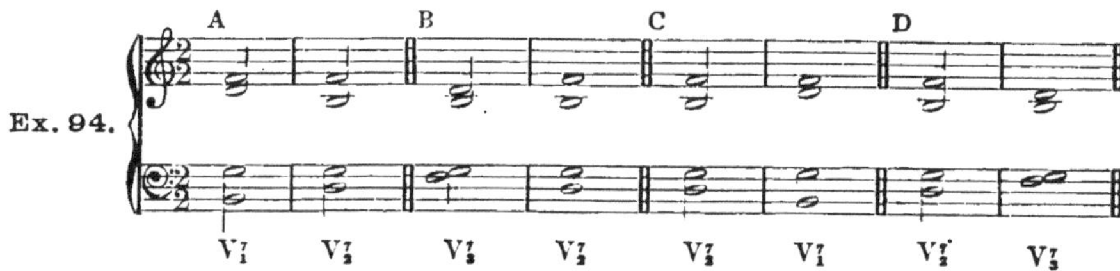


In illustration, Examples *A* and *B* are obviously *not* good, while Examples *C* and *D are* good, satisfying the ear as climaxes in the interrelation of the three inversions. The fundamental position of the $V^7$ chord may become the chord of resolution of either the $V^7_1$ or the $V^7_2$. The $V^7_3$ chord however is seldom used as the chord resolving into the $V^7$ chord, for in such a resolution the bass would have to leap downward the interval of a seventh, which is a difficult interval to sing. The fundamental $V^7$ chord may resolve into, or be followed by, any inversion of the $V^7$ chord.

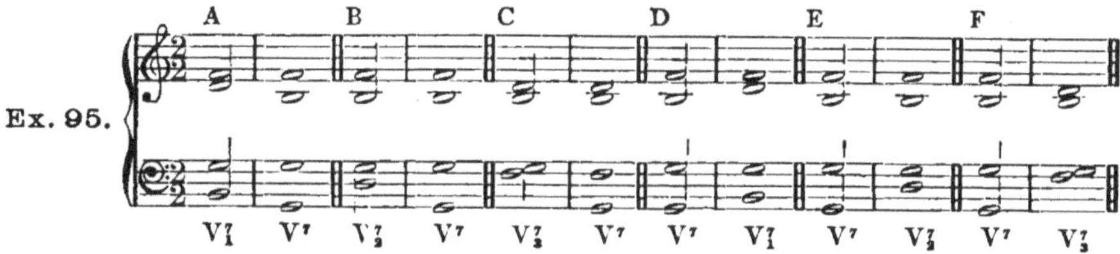


In the illustration above, Example *C* is poor, but Example *F* is permitted. The other examples are often used.

## AURAL PRACTICE

The aural practice of this chapter must include all of the ways of presenting the chords of the previous chapters; and the improvisations using the inversions of the $V^7$ chords must be varied and extensively practiced, for freedom in the use of the dominant seventh-chord and its inversions is most important to acquire. The student should remember, when using the $V^7$ chord in improvisations, that the chord in fundamental position, unless repeated, should be used without its fifth (2nd degree of scale); and when inversions of the $V^7$ chord are used, all tones of the chord should be present. The only way in which the inverted $V^7$ chord ever appears incomplete is in the third inversion ($V^7_3$) when the outer tones, bass and soprano, are so close to each other that there is no room for the fifth of the chord (second degree of scale). For example:

Here the tones of the chord are so close together that the chord-character as an inverted $V^7$ chord is unmistakable; therefore, such a chord-structure is good.

In writing melodies to the given chords of the exercises the melody-tones should always progress, as parts of the $V^7$ chord, in the direction in which they progress in the resolutions of the fundamental and inverted $V^7$ chords. The dominant seventh-chord and its inversions may therefore possess the fifth, seventh and second degrees of the scale, and also the fourth degree, if this degree progresses diatonically downward. In improvisations and melody-writing, take great care not to produce, by the use of the $V^7$ chord, full, perfect and complete resolutions within the confines of the phrases, or at the end of the antecedent phrase. Bear in mind that an inverted $V^7$ chord may be the chord of resolution at the semi-cadence, but that an inverted $V^7$ chord, used as the resolving chord to form the full cadence, is not good. At the full cadence, the fundamental position of the $V^7$ chord should be used for resolving into the I triad in the position of the eighth.

Ex. 97.

In the above illustration, Example *A* may be used as a semi-cadence form. Example *B* is a good chord-relation for use at the full cadence.

The fourth degree of the scale, used as the seventh of the $V^7$ chord, may remain stationary, if employed as one of the parts of a passing-tone chord. These passing-tone chords, as previously mentioned, are generally the second inversions of the triads. For example:

Ex. 98.

In the above illustrations, the fourth degrees remain constantly in the same parts. In Example *A*, in the soprano; in Example *B*, in the alto.

## SUMMARY

The elementary harmonic subject-matter of the major keys has now been discussed, and a general statement as to the method of applying this subject-matter in training the ear is in order.

First, the ear should determine whether a chord is consonant or dissonant.

Second, if consonant, whether the triad is major or minor.

Third, the ear should determine the harmonic activity of the chord.

Fourth, the ear should determine whether a chord is in fundamental position or in an inverted position: (1) by noting the structural activity possessed by the chord; (2) by means of the stepwise diatonic progression of the bass.

The most important use of the ear in apprehending any harmonic subject-matter is to determine the harmonic activity of a chord, thereby being conscious of its relationship to other chords, as it establishes the feeling of tonality, and determines, through its action, the key-centre.

The harmonic relationship of chords to one another is never expressed in the writing of music; such a relationship can only be auralized, for the harmonic relationship of chords to one another demands a different plane from the vertical, represented by music paper, upon which to indicate their action. The vertical plane which is so constantly used in the writing of music is an objective plane, for it is seen that the written tones which act upon this plane represent motion up or down, and to the right, and therefore, in their action they are entirely independent of the position of the person who visualizes their action.

The feeling of key-centre, to which centre all active chords tend in their natural progressions or resolutions, demands that the consciousness be in the hearer who auralizes their action. Each active chord must ultimately be felt to be at a definite distance from and as harmonically progressing or resolving towards the listener. To visualize such an harmonic action, a horizontal plane would have to be employed instead of a vertical plane, for only upon such a horizontal plane can things be visualized as subjectively related. An illustration of the above conclusions follows:

Ex. 99.

The root of the IV triad is here represented as nearer the root of the I triad than is the root of the V triad. Furthermore, the IV triad is represented as being to the left of the V triad, and its root is represented as moving one step upward, and to the right, as it progresses into the root of the V triad. What really ought to be visualized as occurring here is that the IV triad in its harmonic progression should come from beyond the V triad, and harmonically progress into it; and the V triad should be visualized as nearer the I triad than the IV triad. The I triad should always be thought of as the point towards which all the chords tend, and therefore as resident within the hearer himself. If the harmonic law established and written in the first chapter were to be rightly written, the tones composing this harmonic scale would be represented as a horizontal succession of tones, rather than a vertical succession. In this new horizontal position, the key-tone is the representative of the hearer, and each successive tone, the fifth, second, fourth, sixth, third and seventh, would be thought of as being directly back of each other; the fifth the nearest, and the seventh the farthest tone upon the horizontal plane upon which the tones are now represented.

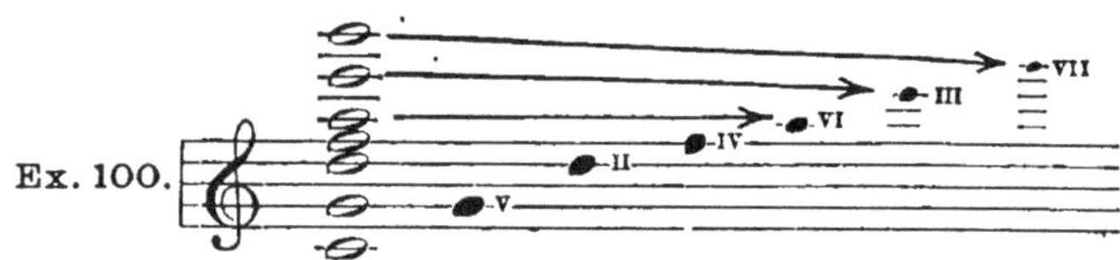


An attempt is made above to show what is implied in this reasoning, by representing the several tones of the harmonic law as changed from the vertical to the horizontal position, in other words, from the vertical to the horizontal plane.

This aural conception, which is virtually the distance from the hearer (I triad), is the more important of the two aural conceptions which are common in music; the horizontal one is the aural apprehension of the harmonic law; the vertical one is the aural apprehension of the melodic law. It therefore follows that the more important of the two laws governing the action of tones in music is never visualized, because it is never written. The only method to be used in becoming conscious of the harmonic law is the aural method. Such is the reason for changing the method of presentation of harmony from the old visual method to the aural method employed throughout this treatise.

It is also seen, that, of the two laws which govern the purposeful action of chords, as they are interrelated, the harmonic law is never changed, nor is it affected by any scale fact. It persists and is permanent; whereas the melodic law is set aside by many facts, such as transferred resolution, diatonic progression, and the like. The melodic law, because of these exceptions to its action, becomes a secondary and supplementary law, and of lesser importance than the harmonic law. In the subsequent chapters upon chromatic harmony it will be found that the melodic law is the law which will be distorted and changed to procure the various chromatic harmonies of a key, whereas the harmonic law will remain unaffected by such chromatic alteration, and the chromatic chord will act in the key in the same way in which it would act if it were a diatonic chord.

Therefore, the student should learn to know a chord through or by means of the law that governs it, and not by any isolated pitch significance which may be attached to the chord; nor is a chord to be discerned by the use of "absolute pitch," which is sometimes part of the intuitive equipment of a musical ear.

Any science finds its beginnings in natural law. The science of music should find its beginning in the same way, as an exposition founded upon logical inductions of a musical science, proved by reasoning, and substantiated by illustrations derived from experience.

It is also apparent as the result of the foregoing chapters that a chord is the servant of the key to which it belongs, governed by the harmonic and melodic laws of the key, and that its use becomes purposeful, determining a definite emotional idea. Such use of a chord, determined through the laws which govern it, must, of necessity, make it purposeful in character and not an isolated euphony, beautiful, but unrelated.

Natural musical composition would therefore result from

the use of chords so related as to express the law which governs them in the most normal or natural manner. Strong affirmation of the harmonic law would result in using a succession of chords whose roots are the successive active steps of the harmonic law proceeding towards the key-centre. A good example of such usage is the Dresden Amen. For example:

The chord-succession in the Dresden Amen is seen to follow the successive steps of the harmonic law as they progress harmonically from the VI triad through the IV, II and $V^7$ chords back to the I triad, resulting in the strong, virile utterance.

## EXERCISES EMPLOYING THE INVERSIONS OF THE DOMINANT SEVENTH-CHORD

3 4 3 6 5 4 3 3 4 2 5 7 8 5 4 3 3 4 3 4 2 1
I $V^7_1$ I IV $I_1$ $V^7_2$ I $I_2$ $V^7$ $V^7_3$ $I_1$ $V^7_2$ I $I_1$ $V^7_2$ I VI $II_1$ $I_2$ $V^7$ $V^7$ I
8 7 6 5 5 4 3 2 1 1 2 1 7 8
I III IV $V^7_2$ I $IV_2$ I $V^7_3$ $I_1$ IV II $I_2$ $V^7$ I
3 4 3 2 1 4 3 1 5 5 4 3 2 1
I $V^7_1$ I $V^7_3$ $I_1$ $V^7_2$ I $I_1$ $V^7_2$ I $II_1$ $I_2$ $V^7$ I
3 2 1 4 3 4 2 7 8 4 3 3 2 1
I $V^7_3$ $I_1$ $V^7_2$ I $II_1$ V $V^7_3$ $I_1$ $V^7_2$ I $I_2$ $V^7$ I
5 6 5 4 3 2 1 4 4 3 2 2 5 3 4 2 7 8 6 2 7 8
I IV $V^7_2$ $V^7_2$ I $V^7_3$ $I_1$ $V^7_2$ $V^7_1$ I V $V^7_3$ $I_1$ I IV V $V^7_3$ $I_1$ IV II $V^7$ I
8 7 8 5 5 4 3 2 2 1 1 3 2 1
I $V^7_3$ $I_1$ $V^7_2$ I $IV_2$ I II $V^7_1$ I $IV_1$ $I_2$ $V^7$ I

3 4 3 6 5 4 3 2 1 2 3 2 1 4 3 6 5 4 3 4 2 1
I $V^7_1$ I IV $I_1$ $V^7_2$ I $II_1$ $I_2$ V I $V^7_3$ $I_1$ $V^7_2$ I IV $I_1$ $II_1$ $I_2$ $V^7$ $V^7$ I
5 4 2 5 7 8 6 5 5 4 4 3 5 6 8 8
I II $V^7_3$ $I_1$ $V^7_2$ I IV I $I_1$ $V^7_2$ $V^7_1$ I $I_1$ IV IV I
8 2 7 8 4 3 3 2 4 3 2 7 8 4 3 1 1 2 7 8
I $V^7_3$ $V^7_3$ $I_1$ $V^7_2$ I $I_2$ V $V^7_1$ I $II_1$ $V^7_3$ $I_1$ $V^7_2$ I VI IV II $V^7$ I
3 2 1 4 3 4 2 3 5 5 1 3 2 1
I $V^7_3$ $I_1$ $V^7_2$ I $II_1$ V I $V^7_2$ $I_1$ $IV_1$ $I_2$ $V^7$ I
8 7 8 6 5 5 5 6 4 2 3 4 3 6 5 4 3 4 2 1
I $V^7_3$ $I_1$ IV $V^7_2$ $V^7_1$ I IV $II_1$ V I $V^7_1$ I IV $I_1$ $II_1$ $I_2$ $V^7$ $V^7$ I
8 5 4 4 3 5 2 3 7 8 4 3 2 1
I $I_1$ $V^7_2$ $V^7_1$ I $I_1$ V I $V^7_3$ $I_1$ $V^7_2$ I $V^7$ I

3 4 5 6 6 5 5 4 4 3 6 7 8 8 7 8 6 5 2 1
5 5 5 1 2 5 5 6 5 5 4 3 2 1
7 8 2 3 4 3 5 6 6 5 5 6 5 7 2 1 5 5 4 3 2 1
5 4 3 2 1 4 3 6 5 4 3 3 2 1
5 5 5 6 7 8 4 4 3 2 1 4 3 2 1 1 1 2 7 8
3 4 2 5 4 3 4 2 7 1 4 3 5 6 5 5

3 4 5 6 5 5 4 3 4 2 3 4 3 2 1 4 3 2 1 3 2 1
I $IV_1$ $I_2$ IV $V^7_3$ $I_1$ $V^7_2$ I IV V I $V^7_1$ I $V^7_3$ $I_1$ $V^7_2$ I $II_1$ $I_2$ $I_2$ $V^7$ I
3 4 3 2 1 7 1 6 7 8 4 3 2 1
I $V^7_1$ I $II_1$ $I_2$ $V^7_3$ $I_1$ IV $V^7_3$ $I_1$ $IV_1$ $I_2$ $V^7$ I
5 5 5 6 6 5 5 4 2 3 2 1 4 3 3 4 3 4 2 1
I $V^7_2$ $I_1$ IV II $V^7_1$ I $II_1$ V I $V^7_3$ $I_1$ $V^7_2$ I VI $II_1$ $I_2$ $V^7$ $V^7$ I
3 2 1 4 4 3 2 1 2 3 4 3 6 5 4 3 2 1 7 8
I $V^7_3$ $I_1$ $V^7_2$ $V^7_1$ I $II_1$ $I_2$ V I $V^7_1$ I IV $I_1$ $V^7_2$ I $II_1$ $I_2$ $V^7$ I
5 3 2 7 1 4 3 3 4 5 1 3 2 1
I I $II_1$ $V^7_3$ $I_1$ $V^7_2$ I VI IV $I_1$ $IV_1$ $I_2$ $V^7$ I
3 2 1 4 4 3 6 5 4 3 5 1 4 3 2 1 2 1 7 8
I $V^7_3$ $I_1$ $V^7_2$ $V^7_1$ I IV $I_2$ $V^7$ I III VI IV I II VI $II_1$ $I_2$ $V^7$ I

---

# CHAPTER XIV

## THE MINOR MODE

Any scale may be considered as possessing two modes (or moods), a major and a minor mode. The major mode of any fundamental tone, or key-tone, has already been discussed. The minor mode of the same key-tone derives from the *under*tones of the fundamental, exactly as the major mode derives from the *over*tones of any fundamental, the process being merely reversed. When the series of undertones of any fundamental tone is established by experiment, and rearranged so as to form a diatonic series, the minor scale obtained will be found to differ from the major scale of the same fundamental by the presence (in minor) of a lowered third and a lowered sixth degree. For example, the minor scale of C will differ from the major scale of C by the presence, in the minor scale of C, of an E flat, and an A flat; all the other tones are alike for both modes of the scale of C. The lowered seventh step occurs as one of the undertones of the fundamental; and in the minor mode, as in the major mode, the tone is raised to procure for the scale an authentic cadence. Therefore, to obtain the minor scale of any fundamental tone, assume the major scale of that fundamental tone, and lower its third and sixth degrees. In so doing, the lowered third and lowered sixth degrees become essential tones of the minor mode of that fundamental tone, and are therefore to be included among the chromatic signs belonging to its signature. For example, take the major scale of C, and lower the third and sixth degrees, E and A; the scale then appears in this form:

The chromatic signs required for the minor scale of C are E♭ and A♭. There is, however, no signature including only E♭ and A♭ in existence, therefore the signature used for the minor scale of C is the major-scale signature in which E♭ and A♭ are found, and which contains the fewest unessentials. This signature is found to be that of E♭ major, for E♭ and A♭ enter that signature as essentials, B♭ being the only unessential included. Therefore, the E♭ major signature is employed for the signature of the C minor scale, and when the tone B occurs as the leading-tone of C minor, a natural sign is written before it to counteract the B♭ in the signature. No signature is employed in A minor, for the first major-scale signature which includes the essential G sharp (the leading-tone in A minor) is the signature of the major scale of A, which also includes the two unessentials F♯ and C♯. Therefore, when writing in the minor scale of A, *no* signature is employed, and the leading-tone is indicated whenever it is required. So it appears that whether writing in minor sharp keys or minor flat keys, the leading-tone must be chromatically expressed.

Hence, the essentials, constant for any minor scale, are the lowered third and sixth degrees; the seventh degree must be raised one half-step in the minor mode to obtain a leading-tone for the scale, and also to make an authentic cadence possible in this mode as in the major mode.

## HARMONIC AND MELODIC LAWS OF THE MINOR MODE

The harmonic law of the minor mode of any fundamental is identical with that of the major scale of the same fundamental. The tones of the harmonic law of any minor scale appear in the same succession as in the harmonic law of the major scale. The tones of the harmonic law are the roots of harmonies in the minor scale, as in the major scale. It naturally follows, that the chord-relationship in minor is the same as in major. Affixed is an illustration of the harmonic law of A minor.

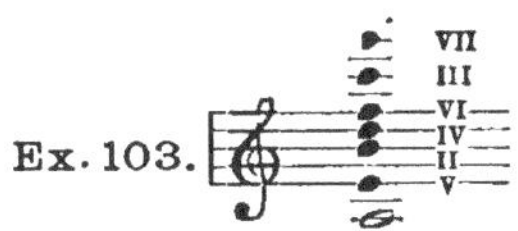


The activities of the tones of the melodic law of the minor scale differ from activities of those of the major scale. This is due to the lowering of the third and sixth steps of the melodic scale to obtain the minor mode of any key-tone. Assume the melodic scale of A minor.

The rest tones in minor are the same degrees of the scale as in major, being the first, third and fifth degrees. In A minor the tones are A, C and E. The other diatonic steps are active tones; the direction and the quantity of their activity are determined, as in the major scale, by the difference in pull in opposite directions of the rest tone on either side of the active tone. It follows, that the activity of the tone B results from the difference between the downward pull of the rest tone A and the upward pull of the rest tone C. The melodic activity of B therefore results in an upward progression into the rest tone C. Likewise, the active tone D progresses in either direction into the rest tones C or E; the active tone F progresses downward into the rest tone E; and the active tone G# progresses upward into the rest tone A. All this shows that the most active degrees of the melodic minor scale are the seventh and sixth degrees; the next less active degree is the second; and the least active degree is the fourth. Because the seventh and sixth degrees are of the same activity, the minor scale is spoken of as possessing two leading-tones. The direction in resolution of the sixth degree is downward, therefore the melodic upward use of this tone into the seventh degree of the scale is against the strongest melodic activity which a melodic tone of the minor scale possesses. And because this upward progression uses the interval of an augmented second between the sixth and seventh degrees, it cannot be called (strictly) diatonic. Therefore, such a melodic progression is not to be used.

## THE PRIMARY TRIADS IN MINOR

The principal or primary triads in minor are the minor triads on the first and fourth degrees, and the triad on the fifth degree, which originally was a minor triad, but becomes a major triad by the raising of the seventh degree, which is its third. The raised seventh degree is necessary in order to obtain a leading-tone in minor, and also that the minor scale may possess an authentic cadence. Therefore, this raised seventh degree may be considered as belonging only to the dominant triad and dominant seventh-chord, as these are the chords which enter into the formation of the authentic cadence. Thus the seventh degree, as it becomes a structural tone of any other chord of the minor key, may be employed in its natural (undertone) appearance, namely as a lowered seventh degree.

The primary triads in the minor scale are interrelated like those of the major scale. The I triad is the rest triad, and is called the key-tone triad. The V triad is the more active of the two remaining primary triads, and is known as the dominant triad. The dominant triad is a major triad in both modes. The IV triad is less active than the dominant triad. It is a minor triad, and is known as the subdominant triad. The primary triads are here illustrated in A minor.

Ex. 105.

The roots of all of the primary triads represented above are doubled to obtain a fourth part, when using the triad in four-part writing. The rule for doubling the parts in the primary triads in minor is, therefore, the same as in major.

In auralizing the primary triads in minor, the student should be careful always to bear in mind that the scale in which the exercise is presented is the minor scale, and that the triads which are minor in the minor scale are the primary triads, remembering that the dominant triad is major in both modes. Therefore, as in major:

First, the character of the triad is determined as minor, major, or diminished.

Second, the harmonic activity of the triad.

## AURAL PRACTICE

All of the methods for employing the practice material in the major mode must be applied in the practice of the minor mode. The given exercises at the end of this chapter use only the primary triads, and are presented in the period length. Triad successions making up these periods are to have melodies added; and improvisations at the keyboard, using only the primary triads, are to be practiced. This keyboard practice is to follow the practice in transposition of these exercises at the keyboard into all of the minor keys.

In writing original melodies using the primary triads in minor as the harmonic basis, the chord-line and the passing-tone melodic forms are still to be employed, with the use of sequence added to procure variety. Caution is to be used in following the melodic activities of the minor mode and not to use the progression flat six, seven at present.

## EXERCISES IN THE MINOR MODE EMPLOYING THE I, V AND IV TRIADS

5 6 5 5 1 2 7 8 5 4 2 3 1 7 2 1
I IV V I I V V I I IV V I I V V I
5 3 2 3 4 1 7 2 5 5 6 4 3 2 7 8 8 4 2 1
I I V I IV IV V V V I IV IV I V V I IV IV V I
8 5 6 5 5 4 2 3 2 3 4 2 7 8
I I IV V I IV V I V I IV V V I
3 4 2 5 5 6 5 5 4 2 3 5 6 4 2 3 4 1 7 2 5 5
I IV V V I IV V I IV V I I IV IV V I IV IV V V V I
2 3 4 2 7 8 6 5 5 6 5 5 8 2 7 8
V I IV V V I IV V I IV V I I V V I
1 2 3 4 2 5 5 4 1 7 1 5 6 5 2 3 4 2 7 1
I V I IV V V I IV IV V I I IV V V I IV V V I

5 6 5 2 3 4 6 5 2 . 3 2 4 3 2 3 4 6 5 5 3 2 1
I IV V V I IV IV V V I V IV I V I IV IV V I I V I
5 6 5 5 8 2 3 4 2 3 4 1 7 1 5 6 5 7 2 1
I IV V I I V I IV V I IV IV V I I IV V V V I
5 6 5 5 4 2 5 5 6 5 4 2 3 4 2 1
I IV V I IV V V I IV I IV V I IV V I
3 2 3 4 1 7 8 8 6 5 5 8 2 3 2 3 4 2 7 8
I V I IV IV V I IV IV V I I V I V I IV V V I
8 7 8 3 4 2 3 4 1 7 8 8 7 8
I V I I IV V I IV IV V I IV V I

## SUMMARY

The minor mode has been spoken of as an artificial mode, because it has seemed to spring from the major mode by lowering the third and sixth degrees in the major mode. There is undoubtedly some justification for such an opinion of the minor mode when looked at from this point of view. There are, however, two points of view which would seem more normal and just, from which to judge the minor mode. These are, first, its historical derivation, second, the emotional aspect of the mode.

The significant tonal feature of the minor mode (versus the major mode) consists in the presence of a lowered third degree and lowered sixth degree. The lowered third degree is the constant and imperative tonal feature. This lowered third degree must remain constant if the mode is to persist. The lowered sixth degree, however, may or may not remain constant in the persistence of the mode, as is shown by the melodic ascending form in which the scale is found. The historical minor scale is in reality one of the modes, so-called, of the Greek system of music, the Hypodorian or Æolian mode. This Greek mode consisted of seven diatonic degrees, beginning on A and ending on A; the half-steps occurred between the second and third degrees, and between the fifth and sixth degrees.

This Greek mode is identical with our A minor scale *without the seventh degree raised;* it is now known as the natural minor scale, and possesses elements of strength and vigor hardly equalled by any other scale.

The emotional qualities inherent in the minor mode are much misunderstood and often misinterpreted. Its emotional meaning should not be one of sorrow or sadness, above all else, not one of weeping and sobbing. The strength that the mode would seem to possess is the strength which results from sadness and sorrow, from experiences which are baffling, uncertain. It would seem to represent the strength which is required to bring out of apprehensiveness a power, to make out *of a veil of misery*, a well. There is that in the minor mode which does not desire (or demand) certainty; therefore it would seem a debatable fact whether the mode should or should not possess an authentic cadence. It is certain that the minor scale written with the lowered seventh step as an ascending melodic step and as an harmonic tone of the dominant chords possesses to a marked degree the emotional qualities spoken of above. Are these qualities the qualities which intense emotions, in fact life in its fullest living, possess? It would indeed seem to be true that the emotional heights and depths of human life are never known except through some deep sorrow, as well as through some deep joy. The life which is lived upon the care-free, happy plane is never the life lived to its fullest measure. The heart which has never known a deep sorrow can never know a great joy, nor can that life ever experience a peace beyond man's understanding. It is this emotional plane or sphere to which the minor mode with its lowered seventh degree belongs, and many passages in the works of the masters point to the belief in the use of the minor mode, thus formed.

It would therefore seem expedient to play for dictation the exercises at the end of the previous chapter, with the lowered seventh degree in the place of the raised seventh degree, in order to give the student the aural estimate of the emotional qualities of the natural minor mode. Fine examples of the use of the natural minor mode are numerous. Such are the opening phrase in the A minor concerto of Grieg, and the last aria of Madama Butterfly.

This emotional aspect of the minor mode versus the major mode is to be referred to constantly when in a succeeding chapter both modes are used in modulation exercise.

# CHAPTER XV

## THE SECONDARY TRIADS IN MINOR: INVERSIONS OF THE PRIMARY AND SECONDARY TRIADS AND THE DOMINANT CHORD

The secondary triads in minor are the triads whose character does not agree with the character of the key; namely, the triads on the second, sixth, third and seventh degrees of the scale. Below are given the secondary triads in A minor:

Ex. 106. 

### THE II TRIAD

The most important of these secondary triads is that on the second degree; in A minor, the triad B-D-F. This triad is a new type of triad-form, namely, a diminished triad. In order to understand its usage, a new line of reasoning is necessary, for this triad-form differs initially from the major or minor triads already discussed, in the significant fact that both of the thirds constituting this triad's structure are minor thirds, B to D, and D to F; therefore the resulting charac ter of this triad is one of unrelationship, for where there is no difference in interval structure, there can never be any relationship implied. The difference in the interval strue-ture of both the major and minor triad-forms is apparent, therefore the root, third and fifth of these triads are easily determined as they are aurally experienced.

This is not found to be the case with the secondary triad on the second degree in minor, in which triad-form both thirds are the same (minor thirds). Hence, the character of the II triad in minor is neither major nor minor, but a new character, namely, *diminished.*

A triad possessing the character of unrelationship can be used, as a serviceable triad, only in that form in which this character of unrelationship is least apparent. Play the triad on the second degree in A minor in its three possible forms, namely, fundamental position, first inversion, and second in-

version: next determine from the resulting sounds which of the forms possesses the least amount of the objectionable unrelated character. The universal opinion is that the first inversion is the only form in which the unrelated character of the triad is so undiscernable as to permit of its use. Therefore the secondary triad on the second degree will appear only in the first inversion, the other forms being discarded as useless, possessing as they do too much implied unrelationship to be of any use.

The parts of an inverted triad are all melodic in character. The parts of the unrelated $II_1$ triad are therefore all melodic in character. In this melodic form of the $II_1$ triad, which part shall be doubled to obtain a fourth? Why is one part doubled in preference to any other part of the inverted triad?

In the case of the primary and secondary triads in major, the character of the triad as related to the character of the key was the principle which determined the part to be doubled. In the case of the $II_1$ triad, no such reasoning will apply, for this triad cannot be said to affirm or contradict the character of the key. The reasoning that does apply in determining which part of the $II_1$ triad is to be doubled to procure a fourth part does, however, take into account the character of the triad, namely, its unrelated character. It would seem expedient to double that tone of the triad which by doubling would tend to lessen the unrelated character possessed by the triad.

The unrelated character of the $II_1$ triad may be obviously lessened by doubling that part which tends to fix or stabilize the triad. All the parts are melodic in character, owing to the inversion of the triad; therefore, by doubling the least active melodic tone of the three which constitute the triad's structure, the above effect is obtained. The least active tone of the $II_1$ triad is its bass tone, which is the melodic fourth degree of the minor scale. Therefore, in employing the II triad in minor, always write the triad in the first inversion and double its bass, not its root.

Although the II triad in minor is harmonically more important than the primary IV triad, it cannot be used as the triad of resolution of the IV triad, for in such a triad relationship the bass tones of the triads would remain stationary (i.e., upon the same degree) over the bar line, and when this is the case (especially in the harmonic relationship of concords), there is not felt to be enough sense of harmonic progression to affirm the harmonic law. It is practically imperative to have the bass voice change over the bar line, in order to feel that an harmonic progression between triads has taken place. Therefore, the IV triad is never used as progressing harmonically into the $II_1$ triad.

The $II_1$ triad, however, is rightly used as a triad harmonically progressing upward into the V triad, or into the $I_2$ triad. It can also progress harmonically downward into the $I_1$ triad, in which case it is necessary to double the fifth of the $I_1$ triad to avoid parallel octaves.

Example *A* is not good, on account of the stationary bass part over the bar line. Examples *B*, *C* and *D* are all good.

## AURAL PRACTICE

In auralizing the $II_1$ triad in minor the triad will sound indefinite and uncharacteristic, and thereby be contrasted with the sounds of the minor and major triads. Its emotional significance springs naturally from its structural characteristics, and the triad has the power to delineate only uncertainty, indefiniteness, unrelationship, chaos, and the like.

### THE VI TRIAD

This secondary triad, in minor, is major in character. Therefore, employ this triad with its third doubled (when possible) in order to de-characterize it, and, by lessening the major quality, make it more adaptable for use in the minor scale. The triad is most often found in its fundamental position. It may, however, occur in the first inversion. The VI triad is very seldom used as a triad of resolution. As a triad progressing harmonically, the VI triad may progress into the IV, the $II_1$, the V, or into the second inversion of the I triad ($I_2$ triad); the first inversion of the VI triad ($VI_1$) progresses harmonically into the $IV_1$.

Ex. 109.

All progressions of the VI triad in the illustration above are good. The $VI_1$ triad is shown in its progression into the $IV_1$ triad.

### THE III AND VII TRIADS

These triads are major triads in the minor key, for in their structure the seventh step is the *natural* seventh step, not the *raised* seventh. Their harmonic use is very limited and takes the form of passing-tone harmonic structure. The III triad is generally found between the I triad and the IV triad (as in the major mode). The VII triad is used as the second triad in a series of harmonic successions remote from the key-centre. A good example of its use is in the opening phrase of the Stabat Mater of Palestrina:

Ex. 110.

Example *A* shows the passing-tone character of the III triad. Example *B* illustrates the use to which the VII and III triads may be put. This kind of harmonic treatment is very seldom employed. The III triad and the VII triad are of as little importance in the minor key as the corresponding triads are in major. Although these triads are major in the minor mode, the roots are generally doubled, for these tones are the tones of the triads most adaptably doubled for the purpose in which they are used, namely, as passing-tone harmonies. One way in which the VI triad may become the triad of resolution of any harmonically progressing active triad is illustrated in Example *B*. Then it becomes the triad of resolution of the VII triad. It may also become the triad of resolution for the III triad. Such harmonic relationships are not advised. The III and VII triads never appear inverted.

### INVERSIONS OF THE PRIMARY TRIADS

The primary triads are found in all inversions. The use of the inverted primary triad in minor is the same as in major. When the triads are in an inverted form, the bass will always be melodic in character. In their second inversion, the V and IV triads are generally used as passing-tone harmonies. The second inversion of the I triad in minor is used exactly as in major, and with the same restrictions.

### THE $V^7$ CHORD AND ITS INVERSIONS

The dominant seventh-chord in minor is identical with the dominant seventh-chord in major, and its use in minor is exactly the same. When the fifth of the dominant seventh chord in the fundamental position is not in the soprano, this tone of the chord is omitted (as in major) for the purpose of employing the I triad into which the $V^7$ chord resolves with all its parts present.

### INVERSIONS OF THE V⁷ CHORD

The inversions of the $V^7$ chord in minor are used exactly as in major, and the rules relating to their resolutions are the same. The practice of the exercise at the end of the chapter is to be conducted in the same manner as in the preceding chapters.

The discussion and reasoning at the beginning of this chapter upon the II triad in minor, obtain for this triad in major; for it is seen that this triad in the major key is the triad on the seventh degree (VII triad). In major, this triad is always used in the first inversion with its bass (not its root) doubled. Its best harmonic progression is into the III triad of the major key.

### EXERCISES IN THE MINOR MODE EMPLOYING ALL TRIADS AND INVERSIONS OF THE DOMINANT SEVENTH-CHORD

1 2 1 1 4 2 1 7 7 8 4 4 7 8 6 4 3 2 7 8
I $V^7_1$ I $IV_1$ IV $II_1$ $I_2$ V $V^7_3$ $I_1$ $V^7_2$ $V^7_1$ $V^7_3$ $I_1$ IV $II_1$ $I_2$ V $V^7$ I
5 5 5 4 3 2 1 4 4 3 3 4 2 1
I $V^7_2$ $I_1$ $II_1$ $I_2$ $V^7_3$ $I_1$ $V^7_2$ $V^7_1$ I VI $II_1$ $V^7$ I
8 7 8 6 5 4 3 3 4 2 1 2 3 4 3 2 1 7 2 1
I $V^7_3$ $I_1$ IV $V^7_3$ $V^7_2$ I VI $II_1$ V $I_1$ $V_2$ I $V^7_1$ I $II_1$ $I_2$ V $V^7$ I
5 5 5 7 8 6 5 4 3 2 1 3 4 3
I $V^7_2$ $I_1$ $V^7_3$ $I_1$ IV I IV I $II_1$ $IV_1$ $I_2$ $V^7$ I
8 8 2 3 4 3 3 2 7 8 6 5 7 8 4 3 3 2 7 8
I $I_1$ V I $V^7_1$ I $I_2$ V $V^7_3$ I IV $V^7$ $V^7_3$ $I_1$ $V^7_2$ I $I_2$ $V^7$ $V^7$ I
3 3 4 2 1 7 8 8 2 3 1 3 2 1
I VI IV $II_1$ $I_2$ $V^7_3$ $I_1$ VI V I $IV_1$ $I_2$ $V^7$ I

1 1 2 7 7 1 4 3 4 2 1 2 3 4 1 2 1 3 2 1
I $IV_1$ $II_1$ V $V^7_3$ $I_1$ $V^7_2$ I IV V $I_1$ $V^7_2$ I IV $IV_1$ $II_1$ $I_2$ $I_2$ $V^7$ I
8 5 6 4 3 2 5 7 8 2 1 3 2 1
I $I_1$ IV $II_1$ $I_2$ $V^7_3$ $I_1$ $V^7_2$ I $V^7_1$ I $I_2$ $V^7$ I
5 6 5 4 3 3 4 3 2 2 1 4 3 2 1 6 5 4 3 4 2 1
I IV V $V^7_1$ I VI $II_1$ $I_2$ V $V^7_3$ $I_1$ $V^7_2$ I $V_2$ $I_1$ IV $I_1$ $II_1$ $I_2$ $V^7$ $V^7$ I
8 7 8 5 5 4 3 2 1 2 3 3 4 5 5 5 8 8 3 2 7 8
$I_1$ $V^7_3$ $I_1$ $V^7_2$ I $IV_2$ I $II_1$ $I_2$ V I VI IV $I_1$ $V^7_2$ I $I_1$ VI $I_2$ $V^7$ $V^7$ I
3 4 3 2 1 2 3 4 4 3 3 4 2 1
I $V^7_1$ I $II_1$ $I_2$ V I $IV_1$ $V^7$ I VI IV $V^7$ I
5 3 4 2 7 7 8 4 4 3 2 7 8 8 2 7 8 8 3 4 2 1
$V_1$ I IV $II_1$ V $V^7_3$ $I_1$ $V^7_2$ $V^7_1$ I V $V^7_3$ $I_1$ VI $II_1$ V $I_1$ VI $I_2$ IV $V^7$ I

8 8 7 8 4 3 2 3 3 4 2 1 7 8
$I$ $I_1$ $V^7_3$ $I_1$ $V^7_2$ $I$ $V$ $I$ $VI$ $IV$ $II_1$ $I_2$ $V^7$ $I$
5 5 5 6 5 7 8 2 1 7 7 8 5 5 4 3 2 1 7 8
$I$ $V^7_1$ $I$ $IV$ $I_1$ $V^7_2$ $I$ $V^7_1$ $I$ $V$ $V^7_3$ $I_1$ $V^7_2$ $I$ $IV_2$ $I$ $II_1$ $I_2$ $V^7$ $I$
8 5 4 4 3 2 7 1 4 3 1 3 2 1
$I$ $I_1$ $V^7_2$ $V^7_1$ $I$ $II_1$ $V$ $I_1$ $V^7_2$ $I$ $VI$ $I_2$ $V^7$ $I$
3 2 1 4 3 2 1 3 2 5 6 5 5 5 4 3 2 1 7 8
$I$ $V^7_3$ $I_1$ $V^7_2$ $I$ $II_1$ $I_2$ $I_2$ $V^7_3$ $I_1$ $IV$ $V^7_2$ $V^7_1$ $I$ $IV_2$ $I$ $II_1$ $I_2$ $V^7$ $I$
5 8 3 7 8 6 5 5 5 5 6 5 7 8
$I$ $VI$ $I_2$ $V^7_3$ $I_1$ $IV$ $V$ $I$ $V^7_1$ $I$ $IV$ $V$ $V^7$ $I$
5 8 2 3 4 3 3 2 7 8 4 4 7 8 6 4 3 5 5 5
$I$ $I_1$ $V$ $I$ $V^7_1$ $I$ $I_2$ $V$ $V^7_3$ $I_1$ $V^7_2$ $V^7_1$ $V^7_3$ $I_1$ $IV$ $II_1$ $I_2$ $V$ $V^7$ $I$

---

## CHAPTER XVI

### MODULATION. — MODULATION TO THE NEAREST KEYS

In the exercises of the foregoing chapters, the fifteen major and minor keys are used. These keys (or tonalities) have been determined as possessing the same diatonic interval relationships throughout, for the major scales and the minor scales, i.e., the intervals between the successive steps of all major scales correspond constantly to the whole and half-steps in the formula 1, 1, ½, 1, 1, 1, ½. These several keys, defined as groups of six tones springing from a key-tone, are in reality isolated groups whose laws are determined by the relationships of the tones and harmonies which they possess, as parts, and as servants. When by any procedure the isolated keys are brought into relation with one another, the fact of modulation occurs. Modulation occurs, therefore, when one key is abandoned and another entered. This is aecomplished by setting aside the harmonic law of one key and setting up the harmonic law of another key. When the harmonic law of one key is abandoned and another one is set up, the ear determines that fact.

Modulation from one key to another is accomplished by the use of a common tone, serving as a tone of junction between the key abandoned and the key entered. The more tones which two keys have in common the closer will be their modulatory relationship. Therefore, the key of C will be most nearly related to five keys grouped around it. These keys are A minor, all of whose tones are common to the key of C with the exception of G♯; the key of G major, the key of E minor, the key of F, and the key of D minor. The major keys of G and F each possess only one tone not common to C major, namely, in G, the tone F♯, and in F the tone B♭. The minor scales of E and D each possess two tones not common to the tones of the scale of C, namely, D♯ and F♯ in the case of E minor, and B♭ and C♯ in the case of D minor.

It is best, while developing a capacity to modulate, to limit the modulations at first to the five nearest related keys above determined, and to enter the new key by a common tone found within its dominant chord (either the V triad or the $V^7$ chord). This method of presenting the new key makes its appearance secure and firmly felt. The key which is modulated from should be closed (or left) for the present upon its tonic triad. A modulation which leaves the old key upon its tonic triad, and enters the new key by means of a tone common to the tonic triad of the old key and the dominant chords of the new key, is the simplest form with which to begin. Modulating from C major into the keys of A minor, G major, E minor, F major, or D minor, according to the above method, is illustrated below:

Here the common tones are shown by the group-marks; observe that the new key always enters by the harmonic relationship of chords *over* the bar line, and that the chord preceding the bar line is figured in the key of the chord of resolution. Also note that the Arabic numeral of the soprano part in the chord preceding the bar line is likewise figured in the key of the chord of resolution. It follows, that modula tion always occurs over bar lines, or at a place where chords are harmonically related.

When the harmonic law of any key is abandoned, two facts may result: First, modulation may occur. Second, a deceptive cadence may enter. Modulation occurs when the harmonically progressing chord belongs to the new key of the chord of resolution. A deceptive cadence occurs when the harmonically progressing chord does *not* belong to the new key of the chord of resolution. Modulation, therefore, sets up a new key, as the old key is abandoned, while a deceptive cadence nullifies all sense of key. The purpose of modulation is to interrelate the fifteen major and minor keys. The purpose of a deceptive cadence is to prepare for modulation by the process of nullifying all key feeling. Examples of modulation and deceptive cadence follow:

Example *A* is a modulation into G major, for the $V^7_3$ chord preceding the bar line belongs to the key of the $I_1$ chord. Example *B* is a use of chords to form a deceptive cadence, for it is seen that the $V^7$ chord preceding the bar line *cannot* belong to the key of the chord of resolution. The triad of resolution is figured as a VI triad in C major, but in reality the triad is a I triad in A minor, and there results from the harmonic relationship of these chords no change of tonality.

The exercises at the end of this chapter are extended to become a two-period form, thereby allowing modulation into all (or many) of the five near related keys to the key of the exercise. In auralizing these exercises, the most important point, to be dwelt upon first, is to group the chords preceding and following the bar line together. Always wait for an harmonically progressing chord to resolve, for only by its resolution will a chord determine its own identity, and also the key-centre to which it is related; for example, a triad which is seemingly reiterated, may not be the same triad, but a triad of a new key, which fact is known only by the harmonic progression of the seemingly reiterated triad.

In all these examples, the triads in the first measures seem to be reiterated I triads in C major, but by virtue of their harmonic progressions they become triads of the keys of the chords of resolution. In each case the harmonic and melodic symbols establish the same fact. These examples illustrate how imperative it is to wait for the chord of resolution before aurally determining the name of the harmonically progressing chord. Always auralize in groups of two chords, which chords are, by virtue of their position in a measure, harmonically related to one another.

The second important point to be dwelt upon is the *character* of the key (whether major or minor) into which the harmonically progressing chord resolves; for according as the new key is major or minor will the harmonically progressing chord be known as a primary or a secondary triad. *B* of the preceding example will illustrate this fact, for the seemingly reiterated I triad there becomes a secondary triad, whereas in examples *A* and *C* the same triad becomes a primary triad.

The third important point is the determination of the melodic degrees of the soprano. This is accomplished by noting the root-tone of any primary triad or dominant seventh-chord, and determining which tone of the chord is placed in the soprano. After determining this fact; the degree of the scale is easily discovered; for example, a modulation from C major to E minor may occur by making the melodic tone C in the alto part of the I triad of C (placed in the position of the third) the tone of junction between the keys, allowing that tone, C, to become the tone in the alto part of the $II_1$ triad in the key of E minor, which $II_1$ triad is then made to progress harmonically into the V triad of E minor, thus:

Ex. 114.

In the above example, the melodic symbol for the soprano tone F♯ of the $II_1$ triad cannot be determined within its strueture. The tone is, however, determined as soon as it is located a third above the soprano tone D♯ of the V triad, which is easily determined as the third of the V triad, by humming the root of the V triad, and writing the tone of the chord in the soprano to be its third, that is, the seventh of the scale. It is seen that the melodic symbols depend upon the chord of resolution quite as much as the harmonic symbols.

The fourth important point is the determination of the *interval of junction* between the soprano tone of the old key, and the soprano tone of the new key; in other words, the *interval of junction* between the keys in the above example representing a modulation between C major and E minor; this interval of junction is the major second formed by the soprano tones of the I triad of C major and the $II_1$ triad of E minor. As soon as the tone of the new key is determined by means of the interval of junction, the melodic numeral above the tone will determine what key has been modulated into, and the succeeding tones are then written in that key. In the above example, the F♯ forms a major second with the melodic tone E of the previous chord, and immediately upon being placed is made the second degree of a minor scale which is easily determined as E minor. In other words, when auralizing an exercise employing modulation, do not try to determine the keys which are used in the exercise until after both laws, harmonic and melodic, have been symbolized. When this has been done, the notes of the soprano part are written in, great care being exercised in determining the *interval of junction* between the soprano tone of the last chord of the old key and the soprano tone of the first chord of the new key. When the soprano tone of the new key is determined, the melodic symbol above the tones should immediately be employed to discover the key which has been modulated into. A suitable form of practice for acquiring facility and speed in discovering the new key is to assume any tone, for example G, and make this tone the second, sixth, third, seventh, fourth, etc., of a scale, and quickly determine the new keys to be F, B♭, E♭, A♭, D, etc.

All of the methods of using the practice material in the previous chapters are to be applied in this chapter, with the exception of the memory work. In this field the exercises would better be divided at least into half, as this phase of the work has, with the entrance of modulation, become very difficult. The improvisational work at the keyboard is, however, most important, and the instructor should aid by taking down improvisations as if the student were dictating to him, and thereby permit a freer use of the material than if the student were required also to memorize what had been improvised. In providing the given harmonic exercises with melodies, more freedom is permissible in the use of figures, rhythmic variation, and sequences. The instructor should prompt this advancement through criticism and suggestion. In improvising new melodies, the student should be cautious to modulate to the near related keys only for the present, and leave the old key on the tonic chord, and introduce the new key by the dominant chord, accomplishing this by allowing the common tone between these chords to be found in the inner parts of the chords, not necessarily in the soprano that is written.

The most important practice of this chapter is the keyboard practice in transposition, and the improvisational work at the keyboard. In transposing, the *interval of junction* between the keys as they appear will be found to be a most important factor. This interval should always be studiously determined. As the Enharmonic Change has not yet been discussed, it is advisable to transpose the given exercise in the extended key-signatures to the simple keys only, for in so doing a knowledge of enharmonic change is not necessary.

The common tone between keys has been determined as the link which joins them. Its presence results in smoothness as one key is abandoned and another entered. This common tone generally occurs in the same part in the chords of both keys. If the common tone is in an outer part (soprano or bass), the resulting modulation will be more obvious than when the common tone is in the alto or tenor. In all cases the other three parts must progress into the chord of the new key in such a manner as not to produce the aural phenomenon of cross relation. Cross relation occurs when a diatonic tone in one part is immediately followed by the same tone ehromatically raised or lowered in another part. For example:

Ex. 115.

The above faulty relationships occur here over the bar line. If such cross relationships occur in the confines of a measure, they are permissible, for in such a relationship of the chords the ear is directed towards the resolution chord, which follows the bar line in its relationship to the chord resolving, and between these chords no cross relationship occurs. The above example would then appear this way·

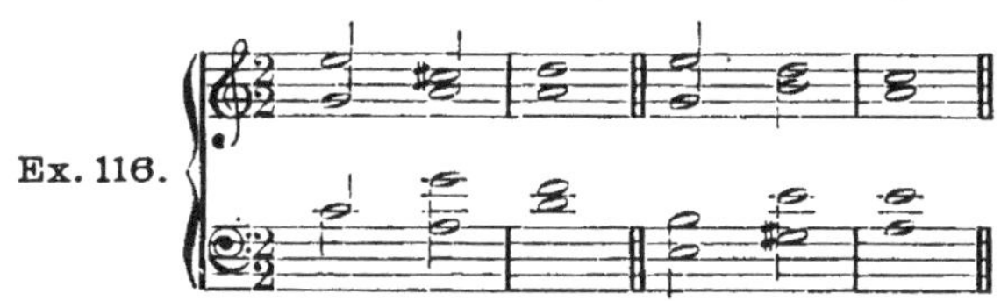
Ex. 116.

However, it is preferable in all cases to allow the chromatic change to occur in the same part in the succeeding key:

Ex. 117.

At *A* it is noted that the common tone, G, appears in the same part in the chord of the new key, namely, the tenor, while all of the other parts progress chromatically. The E♮ and E♭ occur in the same part (soprano) in the chords of both keys. At *B* there is a cross relationship, but, inasmuch as it does not occur over the bar line, as in Example *C*, it is permissible. The cross relationship illustrated at *C* is not good, unless occurring as part of a sequential use of keys. The student, therefore, should endeavor to effect the chromatic changes in the same parts as they occur between modulative keys.

The subject-matter of this chapter has outlined *how* to modulate. It would now seem advisable to inquire *when* to modulate, and what purpose modulation should serve.

It has been remarked in previous chapters that key consciousness is a subjective consciousness, that a key-centre is recognized through the consciousness of the harmonic law, as that law determines the action of harmonies towards the rest triad of the key. The rest triad, namely, the I triad, was found to be situated in the consciousness of the hearer; in other words, the I triad *is* the hearer, discerner, and all other triads and seventh-chords of the key are known by their nearness or remoteness from *him*. This is the consciousness of key, and it is this consciousness which, obviously, is affected by modulation. When, therefore, shall it be expedient and purposeful for modulation to be indulged in?

It is obvious that such a discussion springs only from the psychological phase of the art of music and is in no way determined by a mere desire for variety in composing music. Modulation must have a distinct meaning, significance, and purpose, else its use becomes trivial and meaningless, and merely a matter of euphony, or beautiful sound. Purposeless modulation, which is modulation indulged in simply for the sake of variety, would seem aurally bad in the same way that the use of the color scarlet visually to represent the ocean would be, simply because such a color may be judged beautiful by the artist. If a musical composition is determined as being in a definite key (the key of A, for example), then within that key may be represented the emotional states of mind or heart felt by the composer, as a result of stimuli from without. If this be the case, then, if by his own experience of these emotional states thus acquired he turns them outward towards some individual or reality, he would naturally turn in his emotional experience from the effects of a stimulus towards himself to an emotional experience from himself. The key used in the representation of the emotional experiences *towards* himself may be the original key of the composition, A; the key used in the representation of the emotional experiences *from* himself ought no longer to be the key of A, but some other key nearly related or remotely related to the key of A, as the judgment of the composer may dictate.

The above emotional difference may be represented by the contrasting lines in the text of the motet *Gallia* (the musical setting of which is from the pen of Charles Gounod), "Now behold, O Lord, look Thou on my affliction," and the line "Jerusalem! Jerusalem! Oh turn thee to the Lord thy God!" The first line is an appeal *towards* the prophet, the second line is an appeal *from* the prophet. In the musical treatment of the first phrase by Gounod it will be noted that the key-centre of the (obviously) minor key of E is continuously asserted, evidently to enforce the emotional feelings of the line *towards* the heart of the prophet. The modulation into the major key of D, which immediately occurs at the entrance of the second phrase "Jerusalem! etc." is cleverly prepared by the plaintive reiteration "Jerusalem! Jerusalem!" Its enunciation is still imbued with the sadness and depression which was characteristic of the first phrase in E minor. In the second "Jerusalem" Gounod uses the dominant chord, which is common to both modes, to bridge the transition between the sorrowful and powerful declamation of the first phrase in E minor, and the appealing, hopeful, almost commanding declamation of the second phrase, which occurs in the major key of D. The use of modulation, in contrasting the emotional contents of these lines, is well determined, and the modes (major and minor) are well chosen.

The above illustration is an example of the correct use of modulation, for the choice of keys, and of modes, is evidently justified by the meaning of the lines for which they are employed. Similar justification should always be found for indulging in modulation, and the instructor should constantly refer to the subject, even in the exercises appended to this chapter.

## EXERCISES IN MODULATION, EMPLOYING NEARLY RELATED KEYS

3 4 3 2 1 2 3 5 5 6 4 3 2 3
I IV₂ I II₁ I₂ V I V⁷₃ I₁ IV II₁ I₂ V I
2 4 3 7 8 4 2 3 7 8 2 1 7 8
V V⁷₁ I V⁷₃ I₁ II V I V⁷₃ I₁ II₁ I₂ V⁷ I
3 2 5 4 3 2 3 7 8 4 3 3 2 3
I V⁷₃ I₁ II₁ I₂ V I V⁷₃ I₁ V⁷₂ I I₂ V I
2 7 8 4 3 4 2 3 1 3 4 2 7 8
V V⁷₃ I₁ V⁷₂ I IV V I IV₁ I₂ IV V V⁷ I
5 4 3 3 4 2 3 5 5 6 4 3 2 3
I IV₂ I VI II₁ V I V⁷₃ I₁ IV II₁ I₂ V I
4 2 5 1 2 4 2 3 4 2 3 3 4 3
V⁷₁ V⁷₃ I₁ VI II₁ II V I II₁ V I I₂ V⁷ I

8 7 6 5 ⑤ 4 2 3 7 ⑧ 8 3 2 3
I III IV V7 I II1 V I V7 I VI I2 V I
5 5 ⑤ 4 3 2 3 4 3 6 5 4 2 1
V7 V7 I II1 I2 V I V7 I IV I1 II1 V I
3 4 3 2 1 7 8 7 ⑧ 4 3 3 2 3
I V7 I II1 I2 V7 I1 V7 I1 V7 I I2 V I
4 2 1 4 3 4 2 3 7 8 8 3 2 1
V7 V7 I1 V7 I II1 V I V7 I1 VI I2 V7 I
3 5 ⑤ 2 ⑤ 4 3 4 2 5 1 3 4 3
I V7 I V7 I1 V7 I V7 V7 I1 IV1 I2 V7 I
5 7 8 4 3 1 6 5 2 ① 6 5 7 8
V7 V7 I1 V7 I I1 IV V7 V7 I IV I2 V7 I

5 4 3 5 (5) 4 2 3 7 8 8 3 2 3
I IV$_2$ I V$^7_2$ I II$_1$ V I V$^7_3$ I$_1$ VI I$_2$ V I
5 5 6 6 5 4 3 5 5 5 4 4 2 1
V$^7_2$ I IV II V$^7_1$ V$^7$ I V$^7_2$ V$^7_1$ I IV$_1$ I$_2$ V$^7$ I
5 8 6 4 3 2 3 2 4 (3) 2 1 2 3
I I$_1$ IV II$_1$ I$_2$ V I V V$^7_1$ I II$_1$ I$_2$ V I
4 (3) 3 4 3 2 3 4 3 6 5 4 4 3
V$^7_1$ I VI II$_1$ I$_2$ V I V$^7_1$ I IV I$_1$ II$_1$ V$^7$ I
3 5 (5) 4 3 2 5 3 7 8 8 3 2 3
I V$^7_2$ I II$_1$ I$_2$ V$^7_3$ I$_1$ I V$^7_3$ I VI I$_2$ V I
5 5 (5) 4 3 2 3 5 5 5 4 3 2 1
V$^7_3$ V$^7_1$ I II$_1$ I$_2$ V I V$^7_2$ V$^7_1$ I II$_1$ I$_2$ V$^7$ I

5 4 3 2 1 2 3 7 8 4 3 3 2 3
I $IV_2$ I $II_1$ $I_2$ V I $V^7_3$ $I_1$ $V^7_2$ I $I_2$ V I
2 7 (8) 6 5 5 5 7 2 1 2 1 7 8
$V^7$ $V^7_3$ $I_1$ IV $V^7_2$ $V^7_1$ I $V^7_3$ $V^7_1$ I $II_1$ $I_2$ $V^7$ I
8 7 6 5 5 4 3 2 4 (3) 3 4 2 3
I III IV $V^7_2$ I $IV_2$ I V $V^7_1$ I VI $II_1$ V I
7 (8) 4 3 4 2 7 8 4 (3) 4 3 2 1
$V^7_3$ $I_1$ $V^7_2$ I IV $II_1$ V $I_1$ $V^7_1$ I $II_1$ $I_2$ $V^7$ I
3 2 1 4 3 6 5 5 7 8 4 3 2 3
I $V^7_3$ $I_1$ $V^7_2$ I IV V I $V^7_3$ I $II_1$ $I_2$ V I
2 4 (3) 7 (8) 4 3 4 3 4 2 1 7 8
V $V^7_1$ I $V^7_3$ $I_1$ $V^7_2$ I $V^7_1$ I IV $II_1$ $I_2$ V I

## EXERCISES IN THREE METRE, EMPLOYING THE NEARLY RELATED KEYS

(8) 3 5 6 5 4 3 2 7 8 7 (8) 7 8 4 3 4 2 5 7 8
I I $I_1$ IV $V^7_2$ $V^7_2$ I $II_1$ V $I_1$ $V^7_3$ $I_1$ $V^7_3$ $I_1$ $V^7_2$ I IV V V $V^7$ I
8 7 8 5 5 4 3 2 1 2 3 5 (5) 3 2 1 1 4 3 4 2 3 7
(8) 4 3 3 2 5 5 6 5 5 5 5 8 2 3 4 2 7 8 2 1
$I_1$ $V^7_2$ I $I_2$ V $V^7_1$ I IV V I $V^7_2$ I VI V I IV $II_1$ V $I_2$ $V^7$ I
8 5 4 3 3 4 3 2 4 3 5 5 7 8 8 6 5 5 4 3
I $I_1$ $V^7_2$ I VI $II_1$ $I_2$ V $V^7_1$ I $V^7_3$ I $V^7_2$ I VI IV $I_2$ V $V^7$ I
7 (8) 4 3 4 2 1 7 7 8 7 8 4 3 2 1 1 2 7 8
$V^7_3$ $I_1$ $V^7_2$ I IV $II_1$ $I_2$ V $V^7_3$ $I_1$ $V^7_2$ $I_1$ $IV_1$ $I_2$ $V^7_3$ $I_1$ $I_2$ $II_1$ $V^7$ I
3 4 5 6 6 5 5 3 4 2 3 7 8 4 4 3 3 2 4 3
I $V^7_2$ $I_1$ IV II $V^7$ I I $II_1$ V I $V^7_3$ $I_1$ $V^7_2$ $V^7_1$ I $I_2$ V $V^7_1$ I

(3) 3 4 2 5 4 3 4 2 3 4 3 7 8 4 3 4 2 7 8
5 5 5 6 5 (5) 6 5 4 3 7 8 5 5 6 4 3 2 4 3
I $V^7_2$ $I_1$ IV $V^7_2$ I IV V $V^7_1$ I $V^7_3$ $I_1$ $V^7_2$ I IV $II_1$ $I_2$ V $V^7_1$ I
5 5 5 5 8 4 3 2 7 8 5 7 2 1 4 3 3 4 7 8
I I $V^7_1$ I $I_1$ $IV_1$ $I_2$ $V^7_3$ $V^7_3$ $I_1$ I $V^7_3$ $V^7_3$ $I_1$ $V^7_2$ I $I_2$ $V^7$ $V^7$ I
1 1 2 1 4 3 3 2 5 5 7 (8) 8 3 2 4 3 4 2 3
I $I_1$ $V^7_3$ $I_1$ $V^7_2$ I $I_2$ V $V^7_1$ I $V^7_2$ I VI $I_2$ V $V^7_1$ I IV V I
7 (8) 5 5 6 4 3 2 4 3 4 3 2 5 4 3 2 1 7 8
$V^7_3$ $I_1$ $V^7_2$ I IV $II_1$ $I_2$ V $V^7_1$ I $V^7_1$ I $V^7_3$ $I_1$ $V^7_2$ I $II_1$ $I_2$ $V^7$ I
parallel 5ths good
3 4 5 6 5 4 3 2 1 2 3 7 8 4 3 2 1 1 3 2 4 3 7
I $IV_1$ $I_2$ IV $I_1$ $V^7_2$ I $II_1$ $I_2$ V I $V^7_3$ $I_1$ $V^7_2$ I $V^7_3$ $I_1$ VI $I_2$ V $V^7_1$ I $V^7_3$

(8) 5 5 6 5 4 3 4 2 3 4 3 6 5 5 4 3 3 4 2 1
$I_1$ $V^7_2$ I IV V $V^7$ I $II_1$ V I $V^7_1$ I IV V I $IV_2$ I VI $II_1$ $V^7$ I
4 3 5 (5) 6 4 3 3 2 4 3 2 (3) 3 4 2 3 2 1 7 5 5 7
(8) 5 5 5 4 3 4 5 6 5 2 3 8 7 8 4 3 1 2 7 8
$I_1$ $V^7_2$ $V^7_1$ I $IV_2$ I $IV_1$ $I_2$ IV V V I IV $V^7_3$ $I_1$ $V^7_2$ I VI $II_1$ $V^7$ I
8 7 8 5 5 3 3 4 3 2 3 5 5 8 2 3 5 1 3 4 2 3 2
I $V^7_3$ $I_1$ $V^7_2$ I I VI $II_1$ $I_2$ V I $V^7_1$ I VI V I $I_1$ $IV_1$ $I_2$ $II_1$ V I V
(3) 3 2 1 7 7 8 6 5 5 7 8 7 8 4 3 2 1 3 2 1
I VI $II_1$ $I_2$ V $V^7_3$ $I_1$ IV $V^7$ I $V^7_2$ I $V^7_3$ $I_1$ $V^7_2$ I $II_1$ $I_2$ $I_2$ $V^7$ I
5 1 2 3 4 3 2 7 1 2 3 7 8 4 3 1 2 7 5 5
I $I_1$ V I $V^7_1$ I $II_1$ V I V I $V^7_3$ $I_1$ $V^7_3$ I VI II V $V^7$ I

4 3 3 4 2 5 3 4 2 3 5 2 7 8 4 3 3 4 7 8
V I VI IV V V₁ I II₁ V I V VI V I VI I I₂ V⁷ V⁷ I
3 4 5 6 6 5 5 4 2 3 2 5 4 3 4 2 1 7 4 3
I V I₁ IV II V I II₁ V I V V₁ V I IV II₁ I₂ V V I
5 7 8 4 3 1 3 2 7 8 3 2 3 4 3 1 2 7 2 1
V V I₁ V I VI I₂ V V I₁ I V I IV I VI II V V⁷ I
3 4 3 2 1 1 3 2 4 3 5 5 4 3 5 4 3 2 4 3
I V I V I₁ VI I₂ V V I V I₁ V I I₁ II₁ I₂ V V I
7 8 5 5 6 5 5 8 2 7 8 7 8 4 3 1 3 4 2 1
V I₁ V I₁ IV V I VI II₁ V I₁ V I₁ V I VI I₂ V⁷ V⁷ I
1 2 1 4 4 3 3 2 7 8 7 8 4 3 4 2 1 7 4 3
I V I₁ V V I I₂ V V I₁ V I₁ V I IV II₁ I₂ V V I

---

# CHAPTER XVII

## MODULATION TO REMOTE (OR EXTRANEOUS) KEYS

Modulation having been determined as relying upon the presence of a common tone between the chords of the old and the new key in order to procure smoothness and junction, it would seem that the greater number of tones in common that two keys possess, the nearer modulatively related those keys are to one another. In modulating to remote keys, the presence of a common tone between the chords of the keys will be necessary at present, and the chords will include only these chords of the major and minor modes with which we are familiar. In modulations to remote keys, the key which is modulated from may be abandoned upon any chord and the key modulated into may be introduced by any chord. In modulating from such a key as C major into C♯ major, they would seem to have no tones in common; but upon reflection, it is found that they possess two tones in common, which tones, however, are called by different note-names. These tones are F♮ in C major (which is known as E♯ in C♯ major), and C♮ in C major (which is known as B♯ in C♯ major). When, in the process of modulating, any common tone is known by two names, that tone is said to undergo an "enharmonic change." Enharmonic change is the repetition of one tone in two notations. Therefore, enharmonic change is necessary for establishing a modulatory relationship between certain keys. Many such tones are found in the keys of D♭ major and F♯ major, etc. Such modulations depend upon the presence of a common tone, which common tone simply undergoes an enharmonic change.

A good exercise for practice at this point in the study of modulation is to assume the I triad of the key of C in four-part open position, and successively make the bass, tenor, alto and soprano tones the common tones between the scale of C and all other scales. When the chord vocabulary of the student embraces the chromatically altered chords as well as all the diatonic chords in all keys, modulation will be much easier and smoother. In modulating to remote keys the faulty cross relation of voices is to be carefully guarded against.

In modulation to remote keys, an exercise may utilize many intermediate keys. These keys are not the final or ultimate key towards which the modulation proceeds. Modulation which employs such intermediate keys is said to be transient modulation. A transient modulation is always determined by its fragmentary character, often employing but two chords of the key, and abandoned immediately — the original key again appearing, or some key nearly related to the transient key. Transient modulation is therefore very brief. In establishing a transient key, it is not absolutely necessary to employ the dominant to tonic chord-relation, although such chord-relation is the only one which decidedly establishes the transient key and its mode. The key towards which the modulation proceeds and to which it ultimately comes, must be forcefully and decisively established, and such a modulation is far less fragmentary and fleeting, for, when such a key has been reached, it becomes established by many harmonic relationships, and sooner or later by the V to I chord relationship. Such a modulation is called complete. A complete modulation will employ an entire phrase length at least. A good method of modulation from any key to a remote key is to utilize the change of mode of the key from which the modulation starts. For example, from C major to C minor, or again from C major to F minor; the reverse relationship of these keys (F minor to C major, or C minor to C major) is quite as good.

In the illustration, Example *A* is that of the IV triad of the original key changed from the major triad to the minor triad of the keys of E♭ (as per example), C minor, A♭, or D♭. Example *B* illustrates the I triad of the original key, undergoing a similar change of mode. This second illustration is not in reality a change of key, if the dominant chord were to be used as the chord of resolution.

Such a relationship of chords would exhibit a change of mode of the same key, but not a modulation in the strict sense of the word. The change to minor of the I triad in example *B* (Ex. 118) can readily be made the II triad of B♭ major, the VI triad of E♭ major, also the III triad of A♭ major. In this manner a new set of remote keys is immediately brought into modulatory relationship with the key of C major. In like manner the minor character of the II triad may be changed to major, by raising the third of the triad, and the resulting major triad may become the IV triad in A major, the VI triad in F♯ minor, etc.

The above illustrations represent the type of modulation accomplished without the employment of the common tone.

The first example, *A*, is good, and is much used. The second example, *B*, is less good, as the change of mode makes the modulation much harsher than at *A*. It is apparent that both of these modulations are accomplished by reconstructing a triad of the first key, by changing its character. Any triad of the first key, including the V triad, may be used similarly. Abrupt modulation, i.e., modulation occurring without the presence of a common tone, has a definite significance, and is often employed to outline a sequence, either of a melodic or of an harmonic character. Abrupt modulation is most often introduced upon the strong pulse of successive measures. For example:

Ex. 121.

Two examples of abrupt modulation are, first, the opening of the prelude to *Tristan and Isolde;* second, the treatment of the second theme of the *Aida* March.

The aural exercises at the end of this chapter, as well as those at the end of the previous chapter, are not given as patterns to be followed, but merely as exercises in the auralization of modulation. They are most important, and the schemes for practice employed in previous chapters are to be applied in the practice of these exercises. Great stress is to be laid upon keyboard work, and this practice phase should be confined, at first, to the task of modulating from any key; for example, from the key of C, by using the several parts of the I triad as common tones between the keys, merely intimating the key which is modulated to in fragment. For example, the student is asked to assume the I triad of

Ex. 122.

C major in octave-position, and first use the bass tone as the common tone between the keys to be connected by modulation. To begin with, he is asked to modulate into the key of G; then, into the key of F; then successively into B♭, E♭, A♭, D♭, etc.; then, by enharmonic change of the tone C to the tone B♯, into the keys of C♯ minor, C♯ major, etc. The new key is to be entered, in all cases where it is possible, both by semi- and full effect. The chord of the new key which contained the common tone is to be named by the student before the modulation is effected, and all modulations are to be played as occurring *over* the bar line.

Modulatory improvisations are also to be most extensively done at the keyboard, and in this practice it is advisable for the student to tabulate the cycle of modulation keys which is to be employed, and the manner in which the keys are to be introduced, i.e., by semi- or full effect.

Transposition of the modulating exercises at the end of this chapter is also highly important The student's attention should be directed towards the interval of junction between the keys which will determine the keys modulatively related in transposition, and the new keys thus discovered should be named before the phrase is played. When the exercises are transposed to the so-called difficult keys, for example, F♯ major, D♭ major, etc., the enharmonic change must be freely employed in order not to play in theoretic or fictitious keys.

It is noted in the exercises at the end of this chapter (and the preceding one also) that the modulations which employ the minor modes are marked by a circle placed around the numeral of the melodic law. It is also noted that in some of the exercises there occur chords which have two symbols for both the harmonic and melodic laws; such chords are called "pivotal' chords. They are formed on the weak pulses of the measures, and follow the $V^7$ chord. They become the chord of resolution of the $V^7$ chord, within the confines of the measure, and also harmonically progress over the bar line as an active chord of the new key. For example:

Ex. 123.

4 3 (6) 5
$V^7_2$ I (IV) $V^7_3$

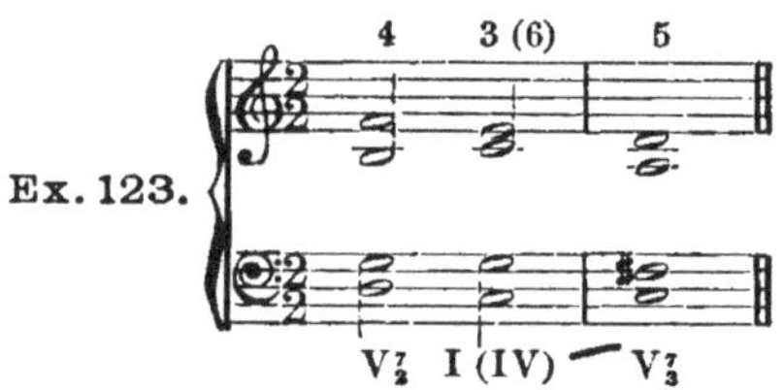

In the above example, the triad on the second pulse of the first measure is a pivotal chord, becoming at once the chord of resolution of the $V^7_2$ chord of C major, and the active IV triad of the key of G major, as it harmonically progresses over the bar line into the $V^7_3$ chord of G major.

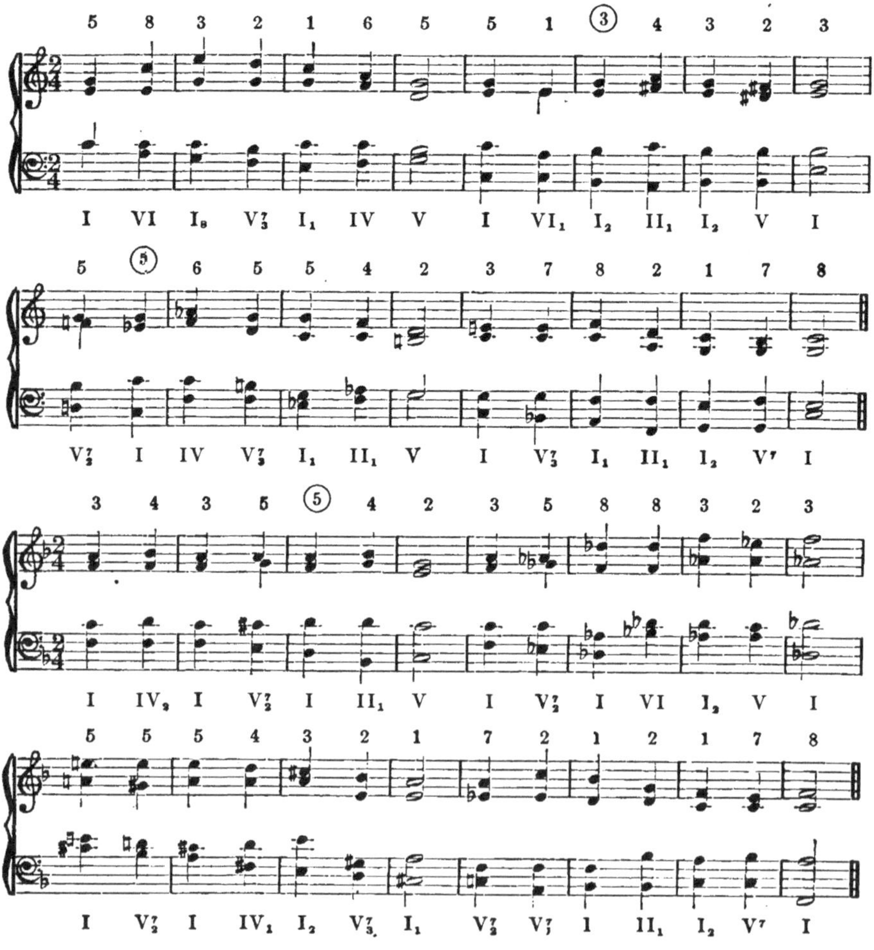
5 8 3 2 1 6 5 5 1 (3) 4 3 2 3
I VI $I_8$ $V^7_3$ $I_1$ IV V I $VI_1$ $I_2$ $II_1$ $I_2$ V I
5 (5) 6 5 5 4 2 3 7 8 2 1 7 8
$V^7_2$ I IV $V^7_3$ $I_1$ $II_1$ V I $V^7_3$ $I_1$ $II_1$ $I_2$ $V^7$ I
3 4 3 5 (5) 4 2 3 5 8 8 3 2 3
I $IV_2$ I $V^7_2$ I $II_1$ V I $V^7_2$ I VI $I_2$ V I
5 5 5 4 3 2 1 7 2 1 2 1 7 8
I $V^7_2$ I $IV_1$ $I_2$ $V^7_3$ $I_1$ $V^7_2$ $V^7_3$ I $II_1$ $I_2$ $V^7$ I

8 8 2 4 3 2 7 8 5 5 1 (3) 2 3
I $I_1$ V $V^7_1$ I II V $I_8$ $V^7_2$ I VI $I_2$ V I
7 (8) 8 6 5 5 3 2 2 5 4 3 2 1
$V^7_3$ $I_1$ VI IV V $V^7$ I $V_7$ $V^7_3$ $I_1$ $II_1$ $I_2$ $V^7$ I
5 7 (8) 4 3 4 (3) 5 5 5 5 5 4 3
I $V^7_2$ I $V^7_2$ I $V^7_2$ I $V^7_2$ $V^7_1$ I $V^7_2$ I $IV_2$ I
(2)
5 8 8 2 7 7 8 7 8 7 8 8 2 1
$I_1$ VI IV II V $V^7_3$ $I_1$ $V^7_3$ $I_1$ $V^7_3$ $I_1$ $I_2$ $V^7$ I
($II_1$)
5 6 5 3 4 4 3 5 7 8 3 3 4 3
I IV V VI II $V^7$ I $I_1$ $V^7_2$ I VI $I_2$ $V^7$ I
5 2 (1) 1 3 7 8 2 7 8 8 3 2 1
$V^7_2$ $V^7_1$ I VI $I_2$ $V^7_3$ $I_1$ $V^7$ $V^7_3$ $I_1$ $IV_1$ $I_2$ $V^7$ I

5 5 5 8 3 2 1 7 (8) 4 3 4 2 3
I $V^7_2$ $I_1$ VI $I_2$ $V^7_3$ $I_1$ $V^7_3$ $I_1$ $V^7_2$ I IV V I
5 7 (8) 8 3 4 2 3 7 8 6 5 5 5
I $V^7_2$ I VI $I_2$ IV V I $V^7_3$ $I_1$ IV $I_2$ $V^7$ I
5 5 5 4 3 2 3 5 5 5 4 3 2 3
I $V^7_2$ $I_1$ $II_1$ $I_2$ V I $I_1$ $V^7_2$ I $IV_1$ $I_2$ V I
5 5 (5) 4 3 2 3 5 2 1 1 3 2 1
$V^7_2$ $V^7_1$ I $II_1$ $I_2$ V I $V^7_2$ $V^7_1$ I VI $I_2$ $V^7$ I
8 7 6 5 (5) 4 2 3 1 (3) 4 3 2 3
I III IV $V^7_2$ I II V I VI $I_2$ IV $I_2$ V I
4 (3) 3 4 3 2 3 4 3 4 2 1 7 8
$V^7_1$ I VI IV $I_2$ V I $V^7_2$ I IV $II_1$ I $V^7$ I

3 5 (5) 7 8 2 7 1 4 (5) 6 5 4 3
I $V^7_3$ I $V^7_2$ I $II_1$ V $I_1$ $IV_1$ $I_2$ IV V $V^7$ I
5 5 5 6 6 4 2 3 5 8 2 1 7 1
I $V^7_1$ I VI IV $II_1$ V I $V^7_3$ I $II_1$ $I_2$ $V^7$ I
8 5 4 3 2 5 5 3 5 (5) 6 5 4 3
I $I_1$ $V^7_2$ I $II_1$ V I I $V^7_2$ I IV V $V^7$ I
7 8 4 3 4 4 3 4 3 6 4 3 2 1
$V^7_3$ $I_1$ $V^7_2$ I IV $V^7$ I $V^7_1$ I IV $II_1$ $I_2$ $V^7$ I
5 4 3 2 1 7 8 7 (8) 8 4 3 2 3
I $IV_2$ I $II_1$ $I_2$ $V^7_3$ I $V^7_3$ $I_1$ VI. IV $I_2$ V I
(8) 6 5 5 (5) 6 5 5 8 8 2 7 2 1
$IV_1$ IV V $V^7_1$ I IV V I VI IV II $V^7$ $V^7$ I

3
1 2 4 3 5 (5) 4 2 5 5 3 2 2 1 5 6 5 5 4 3
I V $V^7_1$ I $V^7_2$ I IV V V I I II $V^7_1$ I $I_1$ IV $I_2$ V $V^7$ I
VI
7 (8) 4 3 3 4 2 5 4 3 8 7 8 4 3 1 1 2 7 8
$V^7_3$ $I_1$ $V^7_2$ I VI IV V $V_1$ $V^7_1$ I IV $V^7_3$ $I_1$ $V^7_2$ I VI IV II $V^7$ I
5 1 2 3 3 4 3 2 7 8 7 (8) 4 3 4 2 1 3 2 3
I $I_1$ V I VI $II_1$ $I_2$ V $V^7_3$ I $V^7_3$ $I_1$ $V^7_2$ I IV $II_1$ $I_2$ $I_2$ V I
5 (5) 4 5 4 3 2 2 4 3 2 1 4 3 2 1 6 6 7 8
$V^7_2$ I IV $I_1$ $V^7_2$ I II V $V^7$ I $V^7_1$ I $IV_1$ $I_2$ $V^7_3$ $I_1$ IV II $V^7$ I
1 1 2 3 5 4 3 4 2 3 4 (3) 4 2 3 3 4 2 5 5
I VI V I $I_1$ $V^7_2$ I $II_1$ V I $V^7_1$ I IV V I VI IV V $V^7_1$ I
8 6 7 8 4 3 3 2 7 8 7 8 5 5 4 3 2 1 7 8
$I_1$ IV $V^7_3$ $I_1$ $V^7_2$ I $I_2$ V $V^7_3$ $I_1$ $V^7_2$ I $V^7_1$ I $IV_2$ I $II_1$ $I_2$ $V^7$ I

8 8 2 3 1 6 5 5 4 3 7 8 4 3 4 2 1 7 5 5
I VI V I I1 IV I2 V V7 I I1 I II II1 I2 V I
(3)
8 2 1 4 3 5 5 7 7 8 3 5 5 5 8 8 3 4 7 8
I I V I V I I1 I I V V I I1 IV1 I2 V7 V7 I
(III)
3 2 1 4 1 3 6 5 4 3 5 8 2 7 8 8 3 2 7 8
I I1 I IV I2 V7 I V IV II1 V I VI I2 V V7 I
5 5 5 6 7 8 4 4 7 8 7 8 7 8 4 3 4 2 7 8
I I IV I1 I1 I I1 I IV II1 V7 I
3 7 2 1 3 4 3 2 4 3 2 5 4 3 4 2 3 2 7 8
I I1 I II1 I2 V I V II1 I IV V I II1 V I
5 5 5 5 6 8 3 2 7 8 4 7 1 4 3 2 1 3 2 1
I V7 I IV IV1 I2 V I1 V7 I1 I1 II1 I2 I2 V7 I

8 5 4 3 2 7 1 4 3 2 5 4 2 1 1 4 1 2 4 3
I I₁ V⁷₂ I II₁ V⁷₃ I₁ V⁷₂ I V V₁ V⁷₁ V⁷₃ I₁ VI IV I₂ V V⁷₁ I
5 5 6 5 5 4 3 3 4 2 3 7 2 1 3 1 3 2 7 8
V⁷₂ I IV V V₁ V₇ I VI II₁ V I V⁷₃ V⁷₃ I₁ I IV₁ I₂ V V⁷ I
8 8 7 8 6 4 3 2 4 3 7 8 4 3 1 1 3 2 4 3
I I₁ V⁷₃ I₁ IV II₁ I₂ V V⁷₁ I V⁷₃ I₁ V⁷₂ I I₁ VI I₂ V V⁷₁ I
5 4 3 4 4 4 3 5 5 5 4 3 2 5 4 3 3 4 2 1
I₁ V⁷₂ I IV₁ IV₁ V⁷ I V⁷₂ V⁷₁ I V⁷₁ I V⁷₃ I₁ V⁷₂ I I₂ V⁷ V⁷ I
3 4 3 2 1 1 3 2 4 3 4 3 2 5 1 2 1 1 4 3
I IV₂ I V⁷₃ I₁ IV₁ I₂ V V⁷₁ I V⁷₂ I V⁷₃ I₁ VI II₁ I₂ V V⁷₁ I
5 6 5 5 4 3 6 5 4 3 7 8 4 3 1 1 3 4 2 1
I IV V⁷₂ I IV₂ I IV V V⁷ I V⁷₃ I₁ V⁷₂ I I₁ VI I₂ V⁷ V⁷ I

# CHAPTER XVIII

## FURTHER DEVELOPMENT OF MELODY: THE ACCOMPANIMENT TO MELODY

In devising melodies formed upon the harmonic bases given at the end of each chapter, the student has become familiar with the passing-tone as an inharmonic (non-harmonic) tone. Passing-tones were found to be tones employed to fill out the harmonic intervals of a chord, thereby inducing a diatonic progression:

Ex. 124.

Here the tones marked × are passing-tones placed between the intervals in the soprano voice of the reiterated I triad. Passing-tones are understood therefore to be tones placed diatonically between two harmonic tones. There are also chromatic passing-tones, which differ from the diatonic passing-tones only in being altered tones of the scale, instead of diatonic tones.

Both diatonic and chromatic passing-tones have to be approached and left by steps and half-steps. Chromatic passing-tones always proceed in the direction of their chromatic sign, sharps upward, flats downward.

Ex. 125.

In the above example are found two chromatic passing-tones, C♯ and D♯, also one diatonic passing-tone, D♮.

A melody may be further embellished by changing-tones. Changing-tones are of two kinds, namely, suspensions and appoggiaturas. The changing-tone differs from the passing-tone in that it can be introduced by a skip, while the passing-tone is always introduced diatonically. The changing-tone, introduced by a skip, and placed upon a strong pulse, is called an appoggiatura. Such a tone immediately joins itself to an harmonic tone. For example:

The melodic tones in the first measure above may have attached to them the marked tones which become appoggiaturas to them, occurring on the strong part of the subdivided pulse. It is seen in the example above that the appoggiatura may be attached to the harmonic tone from below as well as above (above, in the first three pulses; below, in the last pulse). The difference between the appoggiatura appearing above the harmonic tone and the one appearing below the harmonic tone, is, that the appoggiatura from below forms a minor second with its harmonic tone; while appoggiaturas above their harmonic tones may form the interval of a major second or minor second with their harmonic tones. The first kind of appoggiatura shown above gives rise to the chromatic appoggiatura, which appears most generally from below, forming the interval of a minor second with its harmonic tone. For example:

Ex. 127.

Appoggiaturas are sometimes formed in groups where two appoggiaturas are made to relate themselves to one harmonic tone. For example:

Ex. 128.

The tones marked with a × relate to the reiterated harmonic tones preceding and following them. Upon example *B* in the above illustration the following embellishments may also be formed.

This last embellishment generally occurs in but one part, while the passing-tones and appoggiaturas may occur in all parts. In writing melodies to the modulatory harmonic exercises at the end of the previous chapter, the passing-tones and appoggiaturas are to be extensively used, but it must be borne in mind that such inharmonic tones may give rise to faulty part-leading, such as parallel octaves and fifths. For example:

It is noted that the last tone of the passing-tone group is the effective tone in producing these faulty progressions, therefore the student should be cautious about the interval relationship between this tone and the tone to which it is related, and when this interval relationship becomes a perfect fifth or octave, the danger of producing faulty parallel interval progression is present. Care should also be taken not to allow the harmonic tone to appear in the same register as the passing- or changing-tone. For example:

Ex. 131.

The above examples are bad, but the same arrangement of passing-tones and appoggiaturas can occur with the harmonic tone, if the harmonic tone is an octave lower. For example:

### DEVELOPMENT OF HARMONIC ACCOMPANIMENT

The harmonic accompaniment set to the so-called melody of the previous exercises is merely composed of chords. This form of accompaniment consists of the remaining parts of a chord used in four, six, or eight-part choral structure. This same chord-accompaniment may appear in many other forms, and when used in relation to a melody, these forms are called free accompaniments. Some of the forms in which a free accompaniment may appear are now discussed.

First, the chord mass may be repeated in groups of twos or threes, etc., as in the following illustrations:

Second, the tones comprising the chord mass may be arranged to form an arpeggio, as in the following illustrations:

The arpeggio groups may contain as many tones of the chord as desired, becoming, as in the above illustrations, triplets, or groups of four, five, six, etc.

Third, the arpeggio groups may be interspersed with appoggiaturas, diatonic and chromatic, as illustrated below:

Fourth, the tones of the chord may be arranged with passing-tones between them, as in the following illustration:

The figurated accompaniments illustrated in the second, third and fourth divisions, are generally reinforced with chord repetitions in the left hand, in order to enrich them harmonically, and also to make the accompaniment full, thereby supporting the melody to which it is attached.

When figurated accompaniments are used, the rules appertaining to part-doubling in triads, and also appertaining to faulty parallel interval relations, must be strictly observed. For example:

In the above illustration, the figuration in the second measure representing the V triad, doubles the third of this primary triad, which is bad structure. Parallel perfect octaves also arise between the first tone of each group and its harmonic tone, at the beginning of each measure.

Also the faulty parallel perfect fifths arising in the following example are to be shunned:

This faulty progression occurs when the harmony changes, the last tone of the group forming a perfect fifth with the bass tone, while the first tone of the second group forms a perfect fifth with the succeeding bass tone.

The above figurations are only a few of the many which may be used to form a free accompaniment to a melody, but these will suffice to introduce the subject to the student, and it is recommended that these be extensively used when melodies are set to the modulation exercises at the end of Chapters XV and XVI, using the harmonies and the modulations as bases from which to work.

# CHAPTER XIX

## SUMMARY

The triads and dominant-seventh chords, in their fundamental positions and inversions, comprise the harmonic subject-matter included in this volume. The inharmonic tones that have been discussed are the passing-tones and appoggiaturas. Modulation has also been explained and used. It has been deemed wise to separate the above subject-matter from the remaining homophonic material because of the apparent cleavage which obtains at this point in the minds of most students between what is considered elementary harmonic material and advanced harmonic material. There is justification for this division of the homophonic material. Experience in presenting harmony has taught that most minds are able to cope with the triads and dominant-seventh chords, but beyond this point the struggle is a severe one. The triad is a simple chord-structure and therefore does not readily lend itself to many intricate relationships. The dominant-seventh chord is a primary chord, and its structure is also of the type that can in all its elements be recognized intuitively, for the root-tone is instinctively felt by an average musical ear. The harmonic material still to be discussed embraces the secondary seventh-chords and the chromatically altered chords; this material is intricate and given over to involved relationships.

The harmonic material already discussed is of the greatest importance, for it is the basic material of all composition, and ought therefore to be thoroughly mastered before the more intricate material is taken up. Diatonic harmonies are structures built from unchanged law, and are, therefore, elemental and generic; and because harmonic structure is the embodiment of natural and unchanged law, it becomes the fitting vehicle of strong, virile, pure emotions in music. Church music should abound in diatonic harmonic structure, and permit of but little use of chromatic harmony. It would seem imperative, therefore, if one desires to become well grounded in the musical art, that he should thoroughly master the contents of this volume before proceeding to the study of chromatic harmonies, which harmonies initially belong to the secular field of music, and are directly related to the human emotional side of musical composition; for it will be seen that all chromatically altered chords result from changing the diatonic melodic law to become a chromatic law, and therefore have the impress of man's hand upon them.

Another fact to be remembered, as a result of the study of this volume, is the static or resultant quality of triads (concords) versus the dynamic, potent, causal quality of dominant-seventh chords (discords), and through the cognizance of these facts it is expected that all chords, whether concords or discords, will always be used purposefully, and with significant meaning. The euphonious beauty of a chord is not enough reason to warrant its use at any time, and the initial meaning of any chord must take into account the fact as to whether that chord is to be used causally or as a resultant. Discordant harmonies would not seem to have much place in a Valhalla *motif.* The knowledge of the fitting and purposeful use of harmonies is the end and aim of all harmonic study, and this knowledge cannot spring alone from an understanding of the structural facts of a chord, but it must rely upon a full and complete knowledge of the manner in which a chord-structure relates itself to other chord-structures, thereby establishing the laws, harmonic and melodic, through which laws tonality is cognized. In this day, when it would seen that the initial effort of all composition is to destroy all tonal sense, key sense, it is necessary, even imperative, to call attention to the fact that all things are interrelated, that there is nothing in the universe which is isolated or disjoined. Where ignorance of basic and generic law is found, there may seem to be isolated bits of reality, but this seeming unrelationship results from ignorance of the laws which govern those relationships. This, however, cannot be the excuse offered by the musician, for the laws governing the tonal phenomena which he uses are laws well understood, whose actions are fully known.

Therefore, it is required of the musician that he first come into full possession of the knowledge and understanding of the laws of the scale, and if after such an experience he finds it fitting to depart from the laws into the realm of untonality, he will at least do so with a full knowledge of that which he is abandoning and, therefore, he will be more liable to compose in that untonal field with more sense of purpose. The harmonic subject-matter of this volume conduces to much so-called deceptive use, which use is in reality a lawless use. The resolution of the dominant seventh-chord into the triad on the sixth degree is one of the most common deceptive uses to which the harmonic material is put. The deceptive use of harmonies is to be preferred if the purpose of such usage is apparent, and serves the end for which it is employed. Deceptive use of the harmonic material of a key may determine an absolute modulation into another key or a deceptive cadence, in which case tonality is entirely nullified.

CPSIA information can be obtained at www.ICGtesting.com
Printed in the USA
LVOW01s1525080715

445448LV00019B/1004/P

9 781330 294338